Enneagram Type 1

What You Need to Know About the Perfectionist

Your Free Gift (only available for a limited time)

Thanks for getting this book! If you want to learn more about various spirituality topics, then join Mari Silva's community and get a free guided meditation MP3 for awakening your third eye. This guided meditation mp3 is designed to open and strengthen ones third eye so you can experience a higher state of consciousness. Simply visit the link below the image to get started.

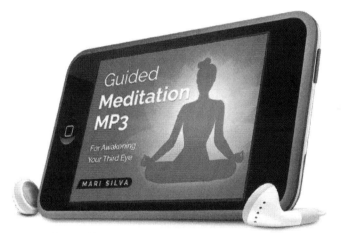

https://spiritualityspot.com/meditation

Contents

Introduction

The Enneagram system of personality analysis has its roots in Bolivia and provides us with useful insights about how different individuals behave and perceive their environments, as well as their interactions and connections with other Enneagram types. This form of study aims to dig deeper into the different colors of our complex personalities and their strengths and weaknesses. This knowledge is necessary to gain a sense of self-awareness to achieve personal understanding and development. It's a system that goes deeper than the everyday astrological signs, which stop at 12 personality types. Through the Enneagram guides, we can find out what is the optimal path for our self-improvement.

Personality Type studies have always been an important element in studying the human psyche by highlighting our unconscious traits and behaviors. When we learn about our primary personality type, we understand the connections between our external and internal experiences and how they influence our behaviors. We are more likely to become better versions of ourselves when we determine and conquer the things we are not aware of in ourselves. We also manage to make more sense of our irritating and unexpected feelings, thoughts, and reactions.

Although there is still some dispute around the accuracy of the Enneagram system, it can't be compared to other theoretical personality studies such as Astrology or the studies of North and South nodes. Why not? Because the Enneagram system is derived from *genuine psychological research and based on proven mental propositions.*

This distinction gives the model its unique perspective and analysis of the similarities *and differences* between human beings. The study of the Enneagram does not touch on the history, intelligence, integrity, or personal skills of individuals. Instead, the system concentrates on disclosing every person's motivational patterns, negative stimuli, and roots. It also goes through the environmental experiences and traumas that may have caused each human being to behave in a particular way.

The Enneagram also teaches us various ways other people around us think and express their ideas. We don't just benefit on a personal level. We also learn about those around us and how we can better communicate with them. Other people experience emotions on different levels and interpret things differently from how we might have thought. This approach is why the Enneagram can help improve our relationships and bring us closer to different types of people around us.

The information covered in this book is in accordance with the contemporary Enneagram teachings, along with the latest discoveries in personality types and human behaviors. So, the book brings you an up-to-date point of view suitable for those reading about the Enneagram for the first time. It also includes direct instructions on identifying your Enneagram Type and using this knowledge to promote self-growth. Along with the detailed psychological discussions, you get to delve into the different psyches of people, discovering the motives behind every human behavior or instinct. These studies help you achieve a special level of enlightenment as you understand yourself deeply and interpret the enigmas of humanity. It's a fascinating journey for your curious intellect, so buckle up.

Chapter 1: What You Need to Know About the Enneagram

The Enneagram system offers us a chance to understand ourselves and our motivation in great depth to help us become better people. The aim is to find the best path possible for every personality type to use for their self-development. There are nine personalities in the Enneagram system. In fact, this is the meaning of the word "Enneagram." It translates to "the nine-pointed figure." It's a system that classifies personality types into three clusters of three types each. Each cluster or center deals with the struggles of the personalities in that group. Although all struggles mentioned are universal human struggles we all experience, some tend to be more prominent in certain Enneagram centers. So, while it's possible to relate to many of the personality types represented in this system, you're going to find yourself relating more accurately to the struggles and patterns of one particular Enneagram type rather than any of the others. So, what is the Enneagram system? Let's dive right in.

Overview of the Enneagram

These studies focus on our childhood traumas and the slow burn of our earlier traumatic experiences, which serve to categorize us into our destined Enneagram types. This could mean we exhibited slightly different personality types as little children. However, we eventually developed our personality types as a result of the subconscious childhood messages we receive. According to the Enneagram, each type implements pre-defined behaviors created to protect them from their core fears found in their Triad center. Each type will also have core desires that they will move toward based on instinctual inclination.

The Triad centers in the Enneagram system are further broken down into the Heart center, the Head center, and the Gut or Body center. To find out what your type is, you need to either learn about the Enneagram or discover each of the nine types so that you can find the one you relate to the most or take the Enneagram test, which gives you a precise result of where you belong in the Enneagram model. Most of the time, your Enneagram type will be the one with the traits and behaviors you're most embarrassed about. It's completely natural for each individual to feel embarrassed or hate their type, and this is because these classifications display the attributes we're most unaware of.

The Historical Background of the Enneagram

Before it was even given its name, the oldest studies of the Enneagram were found within the works of Evagrius Ponticus. This Christian mystic established eight "deadly thoughts" in addition to an overshadowing thought he referred to as The Love of Self. He claimed that every individual's first thought was that of The Love of Self and that the other eight thoughts only followed this primary instinct or thought. He also pointed out eight remedies that are supposed to countermeasure these deadly thoughts.

To follow these studies, the word "Enneagram" and the commonly known figure used in this personality classification system were set down by the Russian philosopher G.I. Gurdjieff. However, Gurdjieff did not develop the Enneagram nine personality types. The contemporary nine types were charted by Oscar Ichazo, who derived these personality categories from some of his teachings revolving around holy ideas, ego-fixations, virtues, and passions. He used his "Protoanalysis" studies that used many ideas and symbols and the Enneagram figure to deliver self-development lecture programs in 1950. He later on minted the term Enneagram of Personality when he founded the Arica Institute in Chile.

The Enneagram Symbol

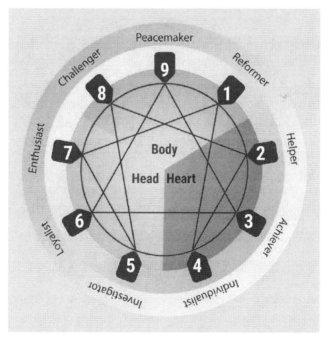

The Enneagram is represented in a geometric symbol with nine points showing along the circumference of the circle. The nine personality types are numbered clockwise from one to nine and allocated with even spaces along the outer circle. Points six, nine, and three are connected by a triangle figure that is located inside of the circle, while the rest of the points on the circumference are connected using an irregular hexagon. In this intricate figure, the shapes inside the circle symbolize how the personality types are divided and connected, while the circle itself embodies the unity and wholeness of human life.

The figure also contains two lines emerging from each basic type to connect it with two other types on the circle. One line connects the type to another type on the circle displaying repressed childhood traits that must be left behind and rejuvenated for the personality type to grow and develop. While the other line for each type is connected to another type that represents the characteristics and traits of the personality that the individual should grow into to achieve the optimal state of maturity and development.

The lines emerging from each type in the Enneagram call attention to the fact that each personality type holds imperative points of strength while possessing tragic challenges that interfere with their lives at the same time. These connections display how personality types can alternate between different traits and behaviors when experiencing different living conditions. It also remolds the descriptive psyche model of the Enneagram and changes it into a dynamic system. To illustrate, Type 1 is connected with Type 7 and Type 4 according to the Enneagram symbol. This means that Ones should move in the direction of Type 7 when facing stress. On the other hand, they need to avoid their negative traits resembling Type 4 to reach full development.

The Enneagram Triads

The three Triad centers in the Enneagram model are considered the most straightforward and indispensable of all the Enneagram Triads. This is compared to the other two Triads in this personality classification system, the Hornevian Triad, and the Harmonic Triad.

There are three Triad centers in the Enneagram figure, the Head center, the Heart center, and the Gut or Body system.

Personality types are grouped in each cluster or center according to their greatest impediment to self-awareness. Our blinding preferences play a huge role in how we inherit and obtain information from our surrounding environments. That said, the Head center groups Types, the Gut Center groups Types 8, 9, and 1, and the Heart center groups Types 2, 3, and 4. Let's examine each center separately.

The Head Center

Types 5, 6, and 7 are individuals who focus on the future, influenced by their sense of logic. These Types struggle with anxiety and worry due to losing their wisdom of the present. When this cluster loses its connection with the present, they tend to build a dissociated perception of their own ego; in other words, The Love of Self. However, they apply this perception differently to any other center by using their sense of ego to find direction and guidance. They rely on themselves and seek security through their unique beliefs and strategies. These types either isolate themselves and internalize their feelings, become conflicted and avoid external threats and internal worries, or externalize their anxiety and escape it through occupying their minds with new activities when dealing with fear.

The Gut Center

This center is subconsciously drawn to the intelligence of the body. However, they struggle with instinctual distortions. The Gut center is made up of Types 8, 9, and 1. Focusing on the body provides us with a direct experience of our livelihood. This essence connects them and helps them become one with their environments. When they drift away from the present, they lose their sense of fullness, confidence, and existing.

The most prominent emotion for this cluster of personality types is anger which transpires from their instinctual response to being hindered or disturbed. They fear losing their essence of intactness and function. Their main concern is gaining control over their environment to achieve order in this disorganized world.

The Heart Center

This cluster struggles with distortions in their feelings. The center includes Type 2, 3, and 4, who depend on their heart and emotions to figure out their identity and discover the truth. They connect deeply with people who resonate with them and open up to those they truly trust. In other words, they use their hearts to identify the quality of their existence and seek the buried truth. Their common emotional patterns revolve around shame, and they seek validation and recognition from those around them. They lacked the capacity of self-reflection as little kids, so they determine who they really are through the eyes and perception of others. This center is mainly concerned with their self-image and seeks attention from their peers. They often experience emptiness, shame, and deficiency when they don't get the attention they expect.

The Enneagram Wings

We've established that the types are located along the outer circle of the Enneagram model with equal spaces and in clockwise order. The types located on either side of your personality type number are called the Wings for your Enneagram Type, and they are the Types you are most connected to. The Wing distinction system is used to prove that each type lies in a vast spectrum, adding more detail, accuracy, and complexity to the Enneagram Personality classification. It implements a rather more intricate strategy that defines people's personality types according to their innate tendencies and life experiences. It's like adding different shades to each personality type to describe it with more precision and thoroughness.

The distinction exists for every type on the Enneagram figure, and it depends on which Wing is more developed for your personality type. For example, if you're a Type 6, you can have a strong Wing 7, which means you're more likely to be easygoing and extroverted. However, you can also have a stronger Wing Five, which means you will be more analytical and introverted than an average Six. So, to sum up, you would still be classified as a Type 6, but you would have different shades to your personality, setting you apart from other 6s. This classification can even influence your character development and shape your personality differently to the point you no longer behave like a 6.

The thing with Enneagram Wings is that your prominent wing does not necessarily have to be the most developed wing. We use the Enneagram system for self-development. It teaches us to work on ourselves by learning the positive aspects of both wings of our specified type to incorporate them into our own lives.

The types on the diagram are not arbitrarily distributed. There is a reason why each number or type is located in its position on the figure. For example, the personality Type Nine is located between the Eight and the One because these people are not always peacemakers who wander through life aimlessly. Nines benefit from their Wing 8 by developing the skill to assert themselves confidently and avoid their fear of conflict. They can also benefit from their Wing 1 by becoming more organized and structured to get more things done and get further along in life.

That being said, it's very important to learn about the types around you when assimilating the Enneagram teachings. The types around you can really help you grow as a person, so make sure you identify your personality type wings when learning about your own type.

The Enneagram's Three Instincts

Our immediate, subconscious reactions to environmental stimuli and activity interactions represent the basic human instincts we have no control over. They constitute the most fundamental part of our everyday life. These are the things we do instinctively without even noticing. The Enneagram aims to group all our instinctual behaviors into three basic classes. These three categories are the Social instinct, the Self-preservation instinct, and the Sexual or One-to-one instinct. These instincts operate within each individual or personality type.

However, they exist with varying strengths. Each type will have one dominant instinct controlling the way they are expressed as a personality.

These variants or instincts symbolize the most superficial layer in any Enneagram Type. To demonstrate, there are three layers to each primary Enneagram Type. So, instincts are the most superficial layer. The layer below that is your main Personality Type, and then comes the deepest layer, which is the Wing of your primary Personality Type. As explained before, this is the Type either to the left or right of your own Enneagram Type.

For example, this is what a complete description of an Enneagram type looks like: Type 1 Wing 9 with a Self-preservation instinct. Given the countless possible mash-ups of Enneagram personality types, including the nine primary types, the two wings for each type, and the three instinctual variants for each type, we get 54 different Personality Type combinations with nine different levels of health for each type.

Self-Preservation

This instinct covers concern for the overall well-being of individuals, their mental health, and their financial security. People with this instinct tend to be disciplined, self-sufficient, and dedicated to self-improvement.

Social

The priorities for this instinct are group involvement and interpersonal relationships. These individuals are very adaptive and tend to have a great sense of social responsibility. This instinct helps them connect with others and understand group dynamics.

Sexual

The sexual instinct covers one-to-one connections, intimacy, and excitement. This Type possesses deep passions and is keen to try new experiences, helping them create genuine relationships with the people they love. They even bind with love itself, seeking chemistry rather than sexual connections.

The Enneagram Test

While you can always read the enneagram type descriptions to know your type, this test helps you get closer to the answer.

When taking this test, be sure to answer as honestly and as spontaneously as possible. Don't overthink the answers, and **do not** choose the sentence that applies to the person *you aspire to be.* Choose the sentence that most represents you as you are now.

This test is a simple game of "this or that." There are two statements in each pairing (#1 has two statements, #2 has two statements, #3 has two statements, and so on).

Read both statements in each pairing, decide which is more accurate for **YOU**, then checkmark the box – regardless of category – in that row. (*Don't worry about the different columns A-I that the boxes fall under!*)

Keep your answers as objective as possible. You'll find the scoring method below the test.

		A	B	C	D	E	F	G	H	I
	When I'm interested in something, it takes my full effort and focus.								☐	
	I prefer keeping things fun and loose.									☐
	I embrace confrontation.							☐		
	Confrontation is not my strong suit, so I try to avoid it as much as I can.	☐								

Statement	1	2	3	4	5	6	7	8	9
I identify as someone who has their head in the clouds.				☐					
I try to keep my decisions realistic and practical.	☐								
I am easily provoked.	☐								
I don't snap that easily.	☐								
People come to me for my insights and wisdom.							☐		
People rely on my decisiveness and strength.					☐				
I know my way around people and can be charming when I need to be.		☐							
I'm a straight shooter and a rather formal person.			☐						
When met with an opportunity, I think about how fun it will be.								☐	
When met with an opportunity, I think about how beneficial it		☐							

will be.									
I find it hard to speak up for myself.				☐					
I will gladly speak up when I have to.									☐
I love meeting new people and expanding my social circle.					☐				
I'm a private person, so a couple of good friends is more than enough.				☐					
I am street-smart. I do my best to survive.							☐		
I have a strong sense of right and wrong, and I stick by my ideals.			☐						
My relationships are my priority.					☐				
I value my relationships, but I won't let them get in the way of my goals.		☐							
I am my main focus.				☐					
Other people will always have my attention, even if it's at my expense.	☐								

	1	2	3	4	5	6	7
Showing affection to people is an integral part of me.					☐		
I'm more comfortable keeping my distance.						☐	
I can put my feelings aside for a job.		☐					
I need to work through my feelings first.				☐			
People think I always know what I'm doing.			☐				
People think I'm rather indecisive.	☐						
I am cautious, and I weigh my options.	☐						
I am adventurous, and I take risks.							☐
I need to be perfect.						☐	
I need to be strong for myself and others.		☐					
I am skeptical, and I follow my head. People might describe me as harsh.	☐						

Statement	1	2	3	4	5	6	7	8	9
I follow my heart and my feelings. People might describe me as soft.					☐				
It's hard for me to loosen up and be flexible.			☐						
Taking action is hard for me. I can't stop considering all possible courses of action and potential outcomes.								☐	
I'm supportive, giving, and I enjoy warmth and intimacy.						☐			
I'm private, serious, and I'd rather spend my time with people discussing issues.			☐						
I tend to hesitate and procrastinate a lot.	☐								
I am often assertive, and I go for what I think is right.							☐		
I'm drawn to asking tough questions and pursuing and asserting my independence.								☐	

Statement	1	2	3	4	5	6	7	8	9
I prefer maintaining my peace of mind.	☐								
My habit of being distant and cold annoys some people.					☐				
My habit of telling people what to do often rubs them the wrong way.				☐					
I prefer comforting people.						☐			
I prefer challenging people and pushing them.							☐		
I'm self-reliant. I rarely depend on people.			☐						
I know I can depend on my support system, and they know I'll be there for them, too.		☐							
I can leave my comfort zone for something I'm interested in.								☐	
I value comfort and security too much to leave them for a pursuit.		☐							

People appreciate my high spirits and humor.									☐
People appreciate my strength and endless support.						☐			
I don't care much for networking or developing people skills. I achieve success by doing the work.								☐	
My people skills have contributed greatly to my advancements and success.		☐							
I pull back in times of conflict.					☐				
Backing down isn't in my vocabulary.							☐		
I love showing off my capabilities.		☐							
I'm uncomfortable showing my skill set.	☐								
I tend to be moody and self-absorbed.					☐				
I can feel removed from reality and preoccupied								☐	

with my thoughts.									
I am usually extroverted and sociable.									☐
I am disciplined, sincere, and serious.				☐					
I feel I am demanding with people.				☐					
I don't put up much of a fight. Others can easily push me around.	☐								
During tough times, I treat myself to a little something nice.									☐
During tough times, I can push aside my problems and keep going.	☐								
I'm always aware of who's trying to take advantage of me.							☐		
I'm constantly looking for the next big adventure and often worry that I'm missing out.									☐
Keeping a "safe and	☐								

comfortable" distance in relationships has caused me many problems.									
My attempts to get people to depend on me recur because of problems in my relationships.						☐			

Each letter corresponds to one of the 9 types. Calculate how many of each letter you got and place that total under "Score." Now, circle the top three highest scores. Your basic Enneagram Type (middle column) is one of those *top three scores.*

Letter	Type	Score
A	9	
B	6	
C	3	
D	1	
E	4	
F	2	
G	8	
H	5	
I	7	

The Enneagram Personality Types

Type 1

Type 1 is the Reformers or Perfectionists who command a lot of purpose and self-control. They are principled individuals who prioritize the security and safety of their environments. Type 1's fear being out of control or incorrect, and often struggle with anger, impatience, and resentment.

Type 2

These are referred to as the Helpers. 2s are very generous and people-pleasing and tend to expect the same from those around them. Sometimes, they can be manipulative or possessive. However, a healthy 2 is always generous and aware of their own needs.

Type 3

The achiever is the type to adapt to most situations; they are driven individuals who excel in most fields. They are also image-conscious and tend to maintain their value through making achievements and meeting people's needs.

Type 4

This type is called the Individualist, which refers to their tendency to isolate when feeling misunderstood or alienated. They are extremely creative and artistic but struggle with feelings of shame or regret. They are also highly expressive and prefer originality which can cause them to feel like an outcast.

Type 5

Investigators are innovative and knowledge-thirsty individuals who never want to stop learning. However, they also struggle with isolation and may appear extremely secretive.

Type 6

Loyalists are engaging and responsible people who struggle with anxiety and suspicions. They are protective of those around them and are completely unaware of their anxious feelings, so they end up struggling to conquer their fears.

Type 7

The Enthusiasts are spontaneous and adventure-loving people, which is what 7s are. They are charismatic, which helps them influence people; they can also become scattered and indecisive when dealing with too many options.

Type 8

8s are Challengers who are full of will and determination. They make firm decisions, love confrontation, and are very self-confident and forthright, making them appear demanding when dealing with others.

Type 9

9s are the Peacemakers. They are open-minded individuals who are generally approving and unaware of their instinctual behaviors and needs. They idealize their environments and relationships to avoid confronting their own feelings of anger.

The Enneagram is a very detailed model that sums up the different personality types of human beings according to their innate traits and instinctual behaviors. It does not just stop at classifying people into nine types. It also explains the behavioral intersections between types and shows their unhealthy tendencies when falling under stress.

Chapter 2: Who Is the Perfectionist?

This chapter focuses on the first Enneagram types and one of the three body types, along with Type 8,- 9,-Type 1, the Perfectionist, or the Reformer. The name describes this type very well. Smart and driven perfectionists who thrive in changing the world around them and finding integrity in everything they do. They have this inner critic inside their minds that guides them to what they should and shouldn't do. However, the world around them is not as perfect as they would like it to be, so they keep trying to make changes. Often, this makes them sound critical and judgmental when they try to correct the actions of those around them. Regardless, you'll see them in a completely different way when you get to know their motives and find out why they behave this way. Let's take a closer look at the typical personality of Type 1.

The Main Characteristics of Type 1

The Compulsive Need to "Be Right"

Although most of the types would have this kind of need, it's rather more constant and persistent with 1s. This type is convinced that being right is somehow the only way of being on top of the situation.

Every personality type will have its own way of viewing the world, and for 1s, being right is the only way of gaining more control over this uncontrollable world. This is why they idolize moralism, absoluteness, righteousness, and arrogance. You'll often hear them expressing how hard they have worked to be right because these are people who do work hard to reach their moral standing. As little children, 1s would put a lot of effort into pleasing their parents and avoiding trouble. They just have to be the perfect kid who never makes mistakes. It's not the worst trait as they always tend to excel at it and impress those around them, not least their parents.

Being Good or Perfect

Not only do 1s thrive on being right, but they also can't accept being anything but "good." They have to be the good student, the good child, or the good employee, which makes perfect sense for a perfectionist to be the best at what they do. So, it's only a matter of time in their lives until they discover that they're not as good as they thought they were. Everybody makes mistakes, but for a Type 1, this is when they start picking on themselves. They are Reformers who constantly try to change imperfections, and so they start by looking at themselves.

They are constantly criticizing themselves for not living up to their own definition of perfection. So, if you think they're judgmental of others, wait until you see how critical they are of their own actions. They will have certain areas in their lives where everything has to be exactly how they want it to be, no matter how silly it may seem. It gives them untold happiness and makes them who they are.

Working Hard

1s only feel good or satisfied when they're making progress or crossing things off their to-do list. They are true workaholics, and you'll see them only taking breaks when they're done. To them, you have to earn your free time or vacation. This is why they look down on people who don't work hard enough to earn the quality of life they're living. There's no such thing as unconditional love to them. People shouldn't get anything for free.

This trait is common for most personality types falling into the Gut or Body Center in the Enneagram. They don't respect people who don't try hard enough because most 1s believe they give their all and work the hardest, although they may only work this hard or dedicate all their effort to a few areas of their lives.

Strong Focus

It's really hard to stop a Type 1 when they're in a flow state. Ones are very focused, and they resent anything that tries to distract them or get them out of "the zone." They try as much as they can to maintain their flow, as this is when they're unstoppable. However, it's also very hard for them to multitask or handle more than one job at a time. They love to have their attention pointed in a single direction, refusing to be interrupted. They'll often seem very serious when speaking as they try to stay concentrated on the given topic. They'll sound focused and stop only when they get their point across.

Meritocracy

1s are highly skilled at keeping lists. Just like Type Two, 1s love to keep count of how much they give, and oppositely, how much they owe or how much those around them owe them. While 2s do it emotionally, 1s do it in a more practical or heady way. As explained previously, they only believe you earn something when you work hard for it. This type of thinking leads them to deeply implement worthiness systems. They have an inner mantra saying, "I deserve, you owe." So, they often sound like republicans looking down on those coming after "a free lunch." Again, this is only driven by their hardworking values that led them to believe that no one else works as hard as they do. They believe the power should only be given to those who put in the effort to earn it, and they're not entirely mistaken.

The Speaking Style of Type 1

1s speak in a very particular way that can be easily distinguished. They are motivated by knowing the right way of doing things. They always seek the best approaches for any particular problem they're dealing with, and therefore, their way of communicating stands out as detailed and organized. They make sure they get their point across and start their conversations by expressing how their approach is considered the ideal approach to the given topic.

For example, you'll hear them starting with phrases like "I figured this is the best way I can explain this." They'll also initiate discussions by sharing their unique knowledge or information and educating others to become more convincing. Ones are extremely precise and honed while speaking. They're also detail-oriented and direct with their language, so you know you're receiving clear and error-free information. They'll just straight up tell you the truth. However, this may be perceived by others as close-minded, sermonizing, or judgmental. This is only because they deliver nothing but the truth and insist on being right. Although sometimes, their information may not be as correct as they think.

When demonstrating their information, they try as much as they can to avoid being showy with their hand gestures or body language. However, if they have to use gestures, they tend to be very clear and precise with them. For example, they would use raised fingers while explaining important points, maybe expressing an underline in a document with their hands, but only when necessary.

The downside of their communication or speaking methods is that they can sound rebuking or criticizing when communicating negative ideas. It can feel like they're scolding you or giving you a lecture, much like a parent-child conversation dynamic.

Childhood Development of Type 1

The Enneagram talks about something called the Wound Theory, which describes an underlying message that we received earlier in our childhood. This message pretty much forms our personalities and shapes the people we are today. Additionally, this childhood message should connect each type to another type during that period of their lives. It is rather related to the concept of the Path of Integration.

For example, a 1's movement to the path of integration is through going to Type 7. What this means is that 1s are used to behaving like 7s as little children. They're not born with the ego of Type 1 as they were only given the essence of this personality type. According to this theory, something may have happened in their childhood years that wounded their essence and made them question who they really are. It gave them the ego of Type 1, just like a 7 would behave when moving into the path of disintegration and becoming more of Type 1. This change in personality does not necessarily have to result from a singular traumatic event; it can be a reaction to a more subtle traumatic experience.

As children, 1s imagine the world as a big magical place where fun and enjoyment can be found just around the corner. They eventually start losing connection with the father figure in their lives or the person who is responsible for providing protection. This is when they start rejecting and losing trust in all authority figures and convincing themselves that they have to create a better environment for themselves. Hence, they perfect everything and reform their surroundings so that they can live in an ideal world.

Unfortunately, they start with themselves. This is when their inner critic arises, causing them never to be satisfied with who they are or what they have accomplished so far. They believe in punishment more than they believe in reward systems. This is because they may have been subjected to an environment where their father figure never celebrated their achievements. They are even motivated to succeed by the fear of wrath rather than seeking achievement. This is commonly referred to as their Foreboding Joy, and they are masters at it.

How Type 1 Falls into the Gut Center of the Enneagram

As explained before, the Gut center or Body center is one of the three Triad centers of the Enneagram. Type 1 lies in the Gut center along with Type 8 and Type 9. As every center represents a principal bias, the Gut center represents the subconscious control of our primal instincts. This is why their bodily instincts move the types within this triad, are focused on the present rather than the future or the past, and frequently struggle with bitterness and anger. This almost sums up the core interests and core struggles of each type in the Gut center.

The Types in this center live in the moment. It gives them a huge sense of fullness, confidence, and, most importantly, existing. However, this makes Anger their prominent emotion. Think about it, these Types' biggest concerns are autonomy and the overall control of their environment. Anger is just an instant response to being messed with or interrupted. For types that thrive on the sense of functioning and getting things done, being interfered with can give rise to a lot of anger.

To relate with the Gut center, Type 1 struggles with rigidness and non-adaptability. Their most distinguished emotions are resentment and judgment. However, on the positive side, they are highly responsible, dependable, and hardworking people. This brings us to the emotional patterns of Type 1.

The Emotional Patterns of Type 1

We can now see how anger is one of the leading emotions for 1s as part of the Gut center. However, to understand how 1s show these angry emotions, we need to go over how each type internalizes or externalizes their emotions based on their location in their Triad group center. For example, Type 8, having a 7 wing from the Head center, would externalize their anger and project it into their outside environments. For Type 1, they would rather internalize their emotions and reflect them inwardly, oftentimes criticizing themselves and being angry at themselves for not living up to their own expectations.

So unlike 8s, 1s would rather hold back their unconscious instincts or impulses. They prefer repressing their anger and internalizing their criticism. This is why they're harder on themselves than they are on others around them. So, in conclusion, 1s do suffer from negative emotions and instinctual impulses, but they just don't like to show it.

The Three Instinctual Subtypes in Type 1

There are three survival strategies that drive the evolution of human beings, known as the three basic instincts. These are Self-preservation instincts, Social instincts, and One-to-One instincts. The first one refers to how we respond to recognized needs and threats, the second one is how we build social structures inside our communities, and the third instinct represents coupling and forming primary relationships. In the Enneagram system, the variation between these 3 instincts is represented differently among each type, which leads to the formation of three subtypes for each Enneagram type.

In the case of Type 1, these three subtypes are as follows:

• The Pioneer, which is the self-preservation instinct for 1s, is driven mainly by their feelings for anxiety.

• The Social Reformer, which is the social instinct of 1s, and which is driven by their difficulty in adapting.

• The Evangelist, which is the one-to-one instinct for Type 1, is mainly affected by zealousness and jealousy.

The Pioneer

It's very important for 1s to conquer their natural environments and achieve order and organization. They engage in material achievements as a way of overcoming their security and survival concerns. They also fear not finding the best approach to resolve issues and will appear either very self-controlled and responsible or anxious and tensed due to self-sacrificing too much.

The Social Reformer

While 1s are gregarious and social in their natural element, they do have their own set of rules. They do not appear as judgmental as you may think, but they struggle to adapt to new situations. Their emphasis on having things done their own way can lead them to resent others and appear critical of those who aren't "correct" according to their own definition of correctness.

The Evangelist

This type may fall into the Gut center for instinctual behaviors. However, they show a lot of self-control with their emotions and instincts in general. They are also highly charged, judging by their Gut center, which leads to overzealousness toward every aspect of their relationships. They insist on keeping their partner's attention to avoid self-remorse. They also experience a lot of jealousy and may even direct it toward people who show more self-expression than them.

Type 1s's Blind Spots

The blind spots are the unconscious barriers in every personality type that most people are not aware of. Most of Type 1's blind spots come from Gut center traits that 1s have no control over or fail to identify as part of their personality. However, once identified these areas that affect. Type 1 can be avoided or changed for the sake of improving relationships with those around them. You can begin to move in a healthy direction and make more peace with others in your life once you find out how to deal with your blind spots and eliminate your negative traits. This is what the Enneagram teaches us, so without further ado, here are the blind spots in the personality of Type 1.

Anger

As a 1, you may have already come to terms with the fact that you get angry sometimes. Most 1s don't realize how much frustration and anger they show with their facial expressions or body language. It's always when someone asks them if they're okay that they begin to realize how angry they actually look or sound. This anger usually comes from their unrealistic expectations for a perfect or idealistic world, just like 7s and 4's.

Over Criticism

While 1s criticize their surroundings and others with good intentions, not everyone likes to be criticized or judged. This is why people consider this a negative trait. Ones do it to find the best approach for doing things; they love reforming their environment. They do it so much that they don't even realize they're overdoing it. Coming from people who don't like to be criticized either, they have to find a way of balancing their expectations so that they don't end up interfering with people's lives or opinions.

Repression of Feelings

1s don't have time to stop or take a break for the feelings of others, let alone their own. They look at emotions as a way of wasting productivity, so they never pay them much attention. This pragmatic way of living helps them get things done, but it's not realistic, and they often break down due to stress. If you're a 1, learn to address your feelings whenever necessary, as repression can eventually cause you to become overwhelmed or lost in your head.

Type 1 Celebrities and Famous People

Famous Type 1s are judicial and principled people who are involved in justice-achieving positions and have a powerful sense of right and wrong. They include:

- The former first lady of the United States, Michelle Obama

- Anti-colonial nationalist and political ethicist, Mahatma Gandhi

- Apple co-founder and CEO, Steve Jobs

- The Canadian singer Celine Dion

- UK's former prime minister, Margaret Thatcher

- Former presidential candidate, Andrew Yang

- Actress, Julie Andrews

- Actress, Natalie Portman

- Actress, Angela Lansbury

- German Chancellor, Angela Merkel

- Former US vice president, Al Gore

- US senator, Elizabeth Warren

- Eleanor Roosevelt, the former first lady of the United States

- Liberal activist and environmentalist Tom Steyer

- And British writer, Clive Staples Lewis

1s are powerful advocates for improvement. They make great teachers, lawyers, and politicians. Even without being involved in these positions, you'll be able to spot a Type 1 in an instant. They are generally distinguishable by their high standards, values, and moralism. However, they can get stuck in their rigidness and lack of adaptability. They're perfectionists for a reason. They have this idealistic image of the world in their heads that motivates them to keep making changes, and that is what they excel at.

Chapter 3: Type 1 — Desires and Motivations

One of the core motivations for Type 1s is striving to always be good and honorable. And this is where we get personal and talk to you, the Type 1. You are motivated by a life of purpose. You are always seeking the most correct and best way to act, which is why this type gets the nickname "the perfectionist."

As a Type 1, you are responsible and keen to live a life of purpose. This is often carried out in a serious and pragmatic way. A lot of your purpose could revolve around improving lives for others and striving to make the world a better place. You often rely on your judgment to come up with solutions that can be used in the real world. Ethics is a big topic for you, and you may find that you spend a lot of time fine-tuning your own moral compass. As and when you come across new information that resonates with your traits, you will naturally adjust.

As part of your purposeful desire, you probably find yourself working hard in the background to make your mission a reality. Duty is a strong value to you, and it comes bounding to the fore, especially in these moments. You are always true to your word and follow through with your commitments because you are so attached to notions of duty. As "the perfectionist," you are always ready to go the extra mile to ensure that the work you do is perfect. Scheduling and organization might be the norm in your life. In every aspect of your life, you are looking to streamline and optimize to fulfill your goals.

You are great at getting things done and don't allow anything to hold you back. You can easily find your direction and head there quickly and efficiently without being sidetracked when it comes to your goals. You find yourself being confident in the choices you make and the things you do. Because you are so efficient, it is important for you to always have something to do because you can execute it so well. Types O1, 8, and 9 belong to the body-based group in Enneagram. This is focused on anger as an emotion. As one of the body types, you tend to become angry when you perceive injustice. This is linked to your core desire to seek a life of purpose; often, the purpose is related to the welfare of others.

You may feel that if you organize everything in your life and retain control, you can avoid experiencing emotions like anger or frustration. As a type 1, you see those types of emotions as being wrong, so you can often find yourself suppressing your emotions. Becoming aware of this is important because now that you are aware, you can begin to see where this happens in your life. If you find that you often feel these emotions but are not sure where they stem from, this could help guide you to the root. As a Type 1, even though you feel anger as an emotion is wrong, it is important to begin to realize that it is an emotion like any other. By expressing it in a healthy manner, you no longer need to suppress it and cause a buildup of anger inside. As mentioned above, this leads to even worse feelings of self-loathing and regret.

Environment

You may have grown up surrounded by a lot of chaos. This kind of uncertainty has caused conditioning that makes you feel like you need to be responsible for having everything together. As a child, when you were surrounded by chaos, you may have begun to feel like the uncertainty could become safety and security by you taking control of the situation. You may have also attempted to control small aspects of your life in an attempt to find stability in the chaos. As an adult, this chaotic upbringing can manifest as perfectionism. You could feel like if you can maintain control and order, everything will be great.

When things don't go your way all of the time, which is inevitable, you could find yourself struggling. That's why it is vital to understand why you have such a need for control. Of course, this level of control is not always a bad thing. It may cause you stress, however, but it can help you to achieve your goals quicker and more easily. Because you love to organize and streamline everything, you can get things done on time. Your commitments are always fulfilled.

Because you are so responsible and strong-willed with the things that matter to you the most, you are able to focus without being distracted. This is one of your greater strengths, as it means that nothing can get in the way of what you set out to achieve. Your confidence in your choices sets you apart from other people. Once you have committed to a decision, you don't doubt yourself but instead see it through to the end. You are fairly naturally motivated, especially when important tasks need to be completed. Procrastination is not in your dictionary.

Honesty

Another one of your core values is honesty, and you expect others to be honest with you. Interestingly, yet another one of your core values is politeness. You feel obligated to be polite at all times. Sometimes when you are honest, it comes off as impolite, and when you are attempting to be polite, it is hard to always be honest.

This can, in fact, cause an internal moral dilemma. A defense mechanism you might use is something called reaction formation. This is where you think or feel one thing, but you behave in the opposite way. You may not be aware of this at the moment that it happens, as it is often an automatic defense mechanism because you have two core values that are in conflict with each other. You don't know how to respond, so you may act outwardly in a way that is the opposite of how you feel inside.

You will usually realize later that you act in a conflicting manner. Unfortunately, this mechanism can put you out of integrity. When you begin to realize this, you can often treat yourself harshly or be quite self-critical. Now that you are aware of the root of this conflict, however, it is easier not to be so self-critical.

Your sense of responsibility is tied up with being honest, but you don't want to treat others in an irresponsible manner. You feel like you have a duty, especially to your loved ones, to treat them fairly and justly. You always want to be upfront and open with your family and friends.

Also, strength is your loyalty. You are loyal to the bone when it comes to your loved ones. You will stand up for them through thick and thin and are not scared to speak your mind, especially if it is something important. If you do have some fears around this, when it is something meaningful to you, you are not afraid to speak out when needed.

Improvement

You are also committed to improving your own life. You are broad-minded in this in that you have a desire to improve every aspect of your life.

You are focused on improving yourself and are always working towards this. Of course, you are just as focused on improving other people and your environment. Your mind is always ready for the next thing you have or need to do. Once you have achieved one thing before you can even take a moment and celebrate, you are already on to the next.

Your value of improvement explains why you feel like you have to leave your work and home environments to truly relax and have fun. However, you could be scheduling and organizing your vacation to such an extent that your vacation stops feeling like a vacation and more like a strict schedule.

Integrity

Integrity has a huge influence on the choices that you make. Some of your other core values include humility, cleanliness, and structure.

In your day-to-day life, you do your best to try and be a person of integrity. You might find yourself standing your ground or refusing to do things others are doing because it contradicts your moral integrity. There seems to be a common thread running through your type of morality.

You aim to be fair and just with others, committed to bettering yourself and others. You are inspired into action due to your deep sense of loyalty, duty, and responsibility.

Justice

Your ideas around justice and how important it is, when paired with your desire to make the world a better place, drive the actions you take. You want a world where everyone is accepted and has equal opportunities. This could be in any aspect, but you are very keen to make your vision a reality.

In whatever role or industry you are in, you have the capacity and drive to make it a safer and fairer environment for everyone. Even if you feel like you have not done anything actionable, you can probably resonate with these ideas and know that you are someone who is deeply seeking a just and fair world. You may feel held back by fear or conditioning. However, this is where you can harness your natural abilities and motivations to work for the greater good.

Careers

You have a lot of important strengths and qualities that are great in the workplace. Some things that make you stand out include your ability to be rational and objective. When decisions and actions are made from a place of subjective opinion, this can cause conflict or issues in the workplace.

You may find that, because of your innate qualities, others look to you as a leader. Because you are less likely to be caught up in the drama, you find it easier to be a neutral, likable individual. Your ability to focus on what is important to you comes in handy as you are able to get the work done, and your perfectionism means it will be done to a high standard.

Because you want to live a life of purpose, you will probably find yourself in a role that provides you with satisfaction and fulfillment. Your desire to be purposeful means that you could spend a great deal of time reflecting on your actions and the way that your actions affect others. It is unlikely you will be someone who is regularly engaged in workplace tension and conflict. Your moral compass will not allow it. Instead, you are a thoughtful and conscientious person.

As a Type 1, you hate to make mistakes and strive only for perfection. This is why working in a place where communication is key is important. Serious, honest, and improvement-focused environments work well for you. This could include a police department or the education sector. You will find yourself thriving career-wise when you work with professionals who are passionate and focused on growing and improving.

Other jobs that would suit you well are the legal profession, architecture, or the police force as a detective. As long as you feel like you are living a life of purpose and can live with integrity and improve the world, you will feel satisfied. You feel a great sense of duty and commitment to spreading what is right. A career that includes all this could work well for you, such as being a therapist, social worker, or police officer.

When you are in an environment that is not right for you, you can be very critical. It can be hard for you to adapt to chaotic or unorganized environments. You should not work in a situation where your ideas may be ignored. This is because this makes you feel like you have no control.

You should also try to avoid a career where you can easily make mistakes, such as in an admin role. Your desire for perfection will be regularly challenged here, and it will be hard for you to feel harmonious and satisfied in such a role. You love to follow the rules and want to have rules to follow. This is why you should not work in places where you are often left to your own devices, as this can leave you feeling frustrated. You need to be able to communicate with others and work in a place where you can organize everything, deliver perfect work, and avoid mistakes or miscommunication.

Because of your desire for justice and purpose, it is best to avoid roles where there isn't an immediate purposeful impact on the work you do. This could be roles like working in retail or serving. You need to feel like what you are doing is making a genuine difference to the world. Of course, you can make a difference in someone's life when working as a server. However, this cannot be quantified or be made certain. It is only a possibility, not something you can verify.

You should avoid careers where you have to be very detail orientated and a perfectionist. This may seem odd considering you have been deemed "the perfectionist," but the pressure of this kind of role means that you can be very critical and harsh on yourself. You will be a perfectionist during whatever role you work, but if you have a career where this is obligatory, it can become too much for you.

In your role, it is important you achieve career satisfaction. For your type, this means working with others who are hard-working, competent, ethical, and responsible. You want to work with a boss who is fair, dependable, and who has integrity. Your work should encourage you to improve situations or aspects you may not notice yourself.

Your career should be one that gives you the ability to work at your own pace so that you can meet the standards you set for yourself. You want to get everything done correctly, rather than just getting it done. You need the time and space to be able to do this in order to feel like you have achieved a job well. Your career should be meaningful and hold value for you beyond the compensation you receive.

Here are some potential careers you might find yourself interested in:

- Political activist
- Warden
- Judge
- Lobbyist
- Monk
- Religious worker
- Clinical psychology
- Librarian
- Inspector
- Accountant
- Auditor
- Writer
- Electrician
- Tailor

These are all varied in terms of industry and role. However, you may find yourself more drawn to certain values that you hold.

Core Values

Here are the core values you hold as a Type 1:

- Ethics
- Duty
- Honesty
- Integrity
- Politeness
- Humility
- Perfectionism
- Structure
- Cleanliness

These are all values that ensure you are a person of morality and integrity. These are important to have as a human being because they ensure that you will always do the right thing. Even in your interactions with your family or friends, you uphold these values. Your strengths can also be your weaknesses; as a Type 1, it's important to give yourself some real downtime in order not to overwhelm yourself. You will begin to experience a build-up of negative emotions and feelings if you do not let yourself take a break from being a high-achiever.

One way to do this in accordance with your Type is to add fun and relaxation to your to-do list. Add this to your schedule so that you can have an immovable time in the day to do something purely for your own enjoyment. Just because you are a perfectionist and can be highly strung, this doesn't mean there are not lots of things you enjoy. Make more time for this so that you have the ability to do all the things you want to and achieve the goals you have set for yourself.

Chapter 4: Type 1 — Weaknesses and Fears

As a Type 1, you set very high standards for yourself. Your core desires revolve around morality and integrity, and you mold your life around these ideals. You always want to be good, and when you fall short of these standards, you feel unworthy. One of your core fears is the fear of being evil or corrupt.

You fear that you could be accused, misinterpreted, blamed, and not meet your standards and expectations. You deeply fear being imperfect, which can make you very frustrated and impatient. You also react like this toward others you consider to be anything less than perfect. This could cause you to become closed-minded, and you may convince yourself that you are always right, which could lead to conflict with others, especially as you cannot move away from black and white thinking.

You could alienate other people by being dogmatic in your thoughts and beliefs. You could be controlling, intolerant, and self-righteous. Because you hold on so deeply to the belief that you are always right, you can often lecture or scold others, and if others ignore you, you could become bitter and angry. As a body-based type, you avoid feelings of anger, which eventually build up in your body. Unexpressed anger eventually leads to resentment and regret.

If you continue like this, it's possible that you start to feel alienated, and that can lead to feelings of depression. You might feel like nobody understands you or your thoughts and beliefs. As a Type 1, you are a committed and dedicated individual. You may have worked hard in order to create an atmosphere of what you understand to be the truth, and if others reject it or don't respond in the manner you want them to, you could begin to feel hopeless and start withdrawing from the world. However, the way in which you begin to feel about the world has clouded you to the point that you wish you no longer had responsibility. Your desire to get rid of your responsibilities is driven by the fact that you would rather fantasize or romanticize a different world. You want the freedom and ease to wish and hope for a world where you and your ideas are received differently.

When you're in this state, if others around you appear to be living happy and fulfilled lives, you can begin to become resentful and envious of them. If you feel like the world has rejected you and you cannot do that, watching others being able to live a purposeful life can cause negative thoughts and feelings. You wish that you, too, could live a life of satisfaction and purpose. When you begin to notice that life is not working for you, you have an opportunity to change it for the better. You may begin to see that your beliefs and ideas could be flawed in some way. This can lead you down a path of self-reflection, and there is space here for you to be able to open your mind a little and move away from your previous black and white thinking.

Much of the reason you fell into this is that you weren't living in accordance with your core values. This led you down a negative path of dogmatism and rigidity. At this point, you might benefit from seeking help from a trusted counselor or therapist. They can help you gently unwind and undo your previous rigidly held ideas. It's important in these moments to take full accountability and responsibility for your life and the actions you have taken. From this point, you can then begin to make big changes. On the other hand, you could continue to feel victimized, which means that your life could begin to deteriorate further. Deterioration could lead to even deeper problems.

You could, for example, carry out destructive behavior but then begin to feel guilty, which will lead you to self-criticize harshly but then act in the same manner again. This turns into a destructive cycle. The reason this happens is that your unconscious drive is at war with your inner critic. You are acting out your suppressed desires and are unable to stop yourself. You might even be carrying out actions that you condemn others for but are unable to stop yourself from doing them.

This is, however, an extreme example of what a Type 1 could deteriorate into if you fall prey to weaknesses and don't lead your life in accordance with your core values. If you allow your critical and rigid side to take over, you will find yourself struggling with life as a whole and unable to stop yourself from carrying out toxic behaviors.

Despite a core fear for you being evil or bad, the above examples illustrate that you could fall into destructive patterns of behavior. One of the reasons why it could be so hard to break out of this is because deep down, you are struggling with not wanting to be bad or evil, and so when you do something that makes you feel like this, you begin to self-criticize harshly. The more this happens, the lower your self-esteem gets. This is how you can get stuck in this destructive cycle. It does not come naturally to you to carry out inappropriate behaviors or actions so, when you do, you feel guilty and consequently bad about yourself. Often though, this happens on an unconscious level. On the surface, you may be acting out because you are having trouble at home or at work, and you need to do something to release the stress. If you do something that deep down makes you feel bad, an inner conflict will begin. Perhaps this will become conscious, but it will manifest as extreme guilt, which leads to a cycle of negative thinking.

It's important to note that these core fears can also be expressed as being someone who does not engage in behaviors that make you feel bad or corrupt. Instead, you might be someone who lives a life much closer to that of your core values. You could avoid any and all types of behaviors that make you feel out of integrity. Of course, this too can come with some issues. You might live a rigid and inflexible life but in a different way. You could find yourself gripping tightly to notions of goodness and morality that you do not allow yourself to open your mind.

Improvement and Perfectionism

As "the perfectionist," you can become fixated on the tiniest imperfections in yourself and others. One of your core desires is to always improve yourself because you are also so focused on being perfect. This desire for self-improvement can become destructive. It is almost impossible to improve yourself to the point of perfection or to the high standards you set yourself. Life happens, and sometimes we do not act or react in the way that we want to. We could be dealing with stress or other life issues, and we are not always our best selves. As a Type 1, it is important for you to truly understand this for you not to fall into a pattern of self-berating when you make a mistake.

Mistakes are normal and are a part of life. No human can escape making a mistake or being imperfect. You could struggle with these ideas even if you know on a cognitive level that this is true. You can easily see that humans are imperfect and that embracing this makes it easier to overcome mistakes. However, deep down, because you are so focused on being perfect, when you do make a mistake, it is almost a subconscious reaction to be so harsh toward yourself.

You can also be harsh on others when they make even the smallest mistake. This kind of reaction can eventually lead to you micromanaging or being controlling in any given situation. This could be at home or in the workplace. In the previous chapter, several strengths were discussed regarding the workplace. Whilst these all hold true, a weakness that could manifest at work is being a micromanager. You might become frustrated with perceived incompetence or mistakes that you become overly controlling. Other people may not be able to carry out their work uninterrupted and could feel that you are overbearing and difficult to work with. You may not even realize that you are acting in this way. To you, you have to act in this way to ensure that everyone is producing perfect work. This section may begin to resonate with you, and you could begin to find that some of your behaviors mirror this. If you think that you have fallen into controlling or micromanaging patterns, take a step back and evaluate how you can change this behavior.

You could also become controlling in the home, feeling like no one else can do chores or tasks the way you can. This could lead you to do everything yourself because you think you can do it better. For a brief period of time, you may begin to feel better because you can see that everything is being done to your high standards; however, as time goes on, you can burn out very quickly as well as become very resentful. Having to deal with every household chore on top of your other responsibilities can become very stressful, especially if you must complete them to an incredibly high standard. This takes up more time and energy, which can deplete very quickly if you take on so much responsibility.

Procrastination

Your perfectionism can lead to procrastination because you are so fearful of making a mistake. When this is not viewed from a rational and objective lens, you can easily continually put off doing anything because you don't want to make a mistake.

Quieting the Inner Critic

Your main weakness is your loud inner critic. This inner critic is always pointing out your mistakes. They have you always looking to perfect yourself, others, and the world around you. This inner critic is almost like a private conversation you have inside, sometimes subconsciously or consciously. Although your inner critic appears to be pushing you toward personal improvement, it is actually manifesting negative thoughts.

Your thoughts massively influence the way you feel about yourself and the experiences you have. Internal negative talk can become incredibly destructive. This is highlighted above were examples of Type 1s who fed fully into their inner critic fell into a harsh cycle of negative behaviors. This inner critic can also be the root cause of low self-esteem or low confidence. If you read over Type 1 core values in the previous chapter and didn't find yourself resonating with many of them, one of the reasons could be that you listen too closely to your inner critic. It can easily cloud your vision, and you could have trouble moving away from the negativity. Now that you are aware of your core values, desires, and fears, you can begin to see where in your life these manifest. These are the areas you should focus on to live a fulfilled life.

The first step to silencing the inner critic is to become aware of your thoughts. For many, our thoughts are happening in the background, a hum as we get on with our day. Tuning into them can feel uncomfortable at first, but the more you do this, the more aware you will become of your internal dialogue. Once tuned in, you can begin to see where many of your actions and feelings come from. Because we might not realize that we have the ability to become aware of these thoughts and then disrupt them, we allow them to affect our lives in a negative way.

The next step is to stop thinking obsessively about your mistakes. As a Type 1, this is how you react to making a mistake. You begin to obsessively think about what you did wrong, constantly reminding yourself of those terrible feelings and thoughts. The more you do this, the worse you feel. Because you are now more aware of your thoughts, you have to stop ruminating on them. One way to do this is to do something to release the tension and stress you are holding onto. This could be in whatever way feels good for you; you might exercise, journal, draw, cook, etc. Anything that might take the edge off, relax you, and pull you into the present moment. If you have difficulty doing this, consider taking up some meditative practices to cultivate presence. The more present you are, the less you will ruminate on your mistakes. Presence prohibits constant cyclical thoughts.

A key step is to question the thoughts you have. An easy way to do this is to ask yourself what you would tell a friend if they were having similar thoughts. The advice you give your friends is usually logical, objective, and rational. This way, you can begin to notice a pattern that the internal thoughts you have genuinely hold little to no truth. They are, in fact, exaggerations of your mind, and these criticisms do not hold true. It might work well for you to examine the evidence around your thoughts. For example, if you just gave a presentation at work but it didn't go as smoothly as you hoped, you could find your inner critic berating you and telling you that you're going to lose your job. Start examining any evidence surrounding this. How did you genuinely do? Did you make a colossal mistake, or did you just not feel as confident as you might have wanted to? Did your boss tell you he was unhappy with the presentation, or did he, in fact, give you positive signs? Did anyone react badly?

Once you begin to examine the evidence, you start to see that actually all of these thoughts are baseless. Sometimes you may find that you could take external circumstances and situations and turn them into something much bigger. A helpful exercise for these moments is to write all the evidence supporting your thoughts. Then next to this, write down all the evidence disproving your evidence. When you come across these overly critical thoughts, begin to replace them with accurate statements. For example, if you think that you did so badly in your presentation that you're going to lose your job. Replace these thoughts with the thought that whilst this may not have been your best presentation, it is certainly not a reason to be fired.

The more you do this, the more you will be able to trust yourself, and you can begin to slowly silence this inner critic.

De-Stress

The easiest way you can avoid falling into your weaknesses is by limiting the number of stressful situations you get yourself into. Of course, because you are a perfectionist and expect the best from yourself, you can often put yourself in situations that make you feel overwhelmed and stressed out. For someone else, they may not be, but because you are so consistently striving for perfection, you can overwhelm yourself. To live a life of integrity and not one of control or rigidity, it is important you take a step back. It is important for you to be able to learn to go for perfectionism. You need to be able to relax and have true downtime. When you can take a break and enjoy yourself, you can avoid being in constant distress.

As a Type 1, you are usually emotion averse and prefer to be practical instead. You may feel uncomfortable focusing on your emotions. However, it is important to do this. You need to be able to express your emotions in a healthy manner. This will allow you to let go of much of your stress and tension. You can prevent burnout and overwhelm by finding a way to healthily channel your behavior. When you can rid yourself of constantly being overly critical of yourself and others, you can allow yourself to live a life of purpose and responsibility. It is important for you to find the right balance that allows you to find purpose, help others, and yourself while also not relying heavily on your inner critic.

Chapter 5: Unhealthy 1s: The Path of Disintegration

One thing most people don't realize about the Enneagram model of personality is that it is not a static model. Instead, the symbol of the Enneagram represents the way that people can change over time.

If you've ever seen the symbol of the Enneagram, you've probably noticed the lines within the circle connecting the personality points in the circle's perimeter. Though they may seem like random and arbitrary lines, this couldn't be further from the truth.

Instead, the lines provide a map of how each personality type will react in certain situations.

If you pay close attention to the symbol, you will notice that each personality type is linked to two other personality types. One of these links represents how a healthy person reacts to situations and how their personality grows and develops. This is known as the Direction of Integration or the Direction of Growth.

The second line, however, is a different matter. Instead of representing the person's growth, it indicates how they will react in stressful, pressure-filled situations or when they feel they are quickly losing control. This also explains the reaction of an unhealthy personality to difficult moments in their life, and is known as the Direction of Stress, or the Direction of Disintegration.

The Levels of Development

The Levels of Development is a theory posited by Riso and Hudson from the Enneagram institute to further explain why a person's personality shifts over time – and why they choose one path over the other.

The theory posits that all people fall into one of nine levels of functioning. They're usually divided into healthy levels (1 3 One to Three), average levels (4 6 Four to Six), and unhealthy levels (7 9 Seven to Nine).

To understand this theory better, let's look at each of the nine levels in a little more detail. The model posits that most people move, on average, up from Level Nine to Level One.

> • **Level Nine:** This level is the level of pathological destructiveness. Most people experience this level at least once in their lives – when they are infants. Infants are purely interested in their inner reality and basic needs – and are wholly disconnected from society. They care only about their own comfort and are demanding of their caretakers without giving anything back in return. While this is a normal and healthy state for babies and infants, this is extremely unhealthy for adults. Most adults at this level present with psychopathy or severe developmental disabilities.

> • **Level Eight:** This is the level of delusion and compulsion. In children, it can be seen as they learn through repetition. However, as with Level Nine, what is normal for children is disordered behavior in an adult. While a child may believe in the illusion of Santa Claus or the Easter Bunny, for example, adults

believing in similar delusions or exhibiting compulsive and repetitive behavior is a sign of a major personality disorder, addiction, or major anxiety.

- **Level Seven:** This is the level of violation. In children, it involves the child being demanding, uncaring, or not respecting personal boundaries, and "grabby." However, again, what is normal for a toddler is not appropriate for an adult. Screaming, hitting, and biting are no longer acceptable behaviors. Adults who display such tendencies are often either neurotic – or relying on the behavior as a survival tactic due to abuse or trauma.

- **Level Six:** This is the level of overcompensation. In children, it is the movement from violence to becoming more comfortable using their words to articulate demands. In adults, it represents authoritarianism, conflict with others, and a desire to advance one's own ego to the detriment of others.

- **Level Five:** This is the level of interpersonal control. It represents the development of problem-solving capacity in younger children and sees them engaging in conflict with others to determine who will win. With adults, it can result in manipulation of others or defensive behavior. This level often corresponds with individualism and a desire for autonomy.

- **Level Four:** This is the level of imbalance. At this level, personality movement is more conscious than it is natural, especially earlier in life. At this level, people work to get their inner critics off the backs and try to reach their ego ideals. It is the level at which defenses are raised, and people start moving toward their aspirational ego roles.

- **Level Three:** This is the level of social value. People begin to appreciate their role as individuals in society as a larger whole, and they start to better understand their purpose in life. At this level, the ego is operating constructively.

- **Level Two:** This is the level of psychological capacity. This requires people to do challenging work on understanding themselves, often at the spiritual level. At this level, the ego has reached the person's ideal self.

- **Level One:** This is the level of liberation. It involves facing your deepest fears and truly being able to understand yourself as a person. While you reach your ideal self at Level Two, you transcend this ideal and find total internal freedom at Level One.

Given the standard distribution curve, the theory is that most people (68%) fall in the average level (4-6). Levels T3 -3 to 7 account for about 95% of people. The remaining five% fall on the extremes – Levels 1 - 2, or Levels 8 -9.

Levels of Development and the Enneagram

As discussed above, the Enneagram accounts for personality shifts. The Levels of Development theory maps out those personality shifts – people who fall on Levels 1 - 3 are on the Direction of Integration, while those on Level 7 - 9 share on the Direction of Disintegration.

Remember, these directions – also known as movement points – are not static. It is possible for a person to move from the Direction of Integration to the Direction of Disintegration and vice versa. By having a better idea of what these paths entail, you'll be able to stave off disintegration and instead take steps towards personality growth.

Understanding Movement Points

The movement points represent the path that a person takes by showing exactly how their personality type integrates or disintegrates. No matter which path you follow, it involves taking on the healthy (or unhealthy, depending on the direction you're on) traits from another personality type.

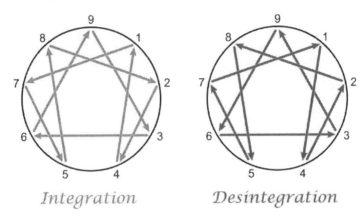

Integration   *Desintegration*

The personality types linked by the movement points explain which traits you are likely to take on. As a Perfectionist and Personality Type 1, when you are in the Direction of Integration, you will take on the positive traits of 7s. This means you become more forgiving of yourself, are more open, and start to pay attention to the positives around you.

Similarly, 2s integrate to 4s, 3s to 6, 4s to 1s, and 5s to 8s. Furthermore, 6s integrate to 9s, 7s to 5s, 8s to 2s, and 9s to 3s.

As with integration, the path of disintegration is laid out as well. As a Personality Type 1, when you are in the Direction of Disintegration, you will take on the negative traits of 4s. You will become angrier with yourself, lose self-esteem, and start to feel unloved and hopeless.

Similarly, 2s disintegrate to 8s, 3s to 9s, 4s to 2s, and 5s to 7s. Additionally, 6s disintegrate to 3s, 7s to 1s, 8s to 5s, and 9s to 6s.

In this chapter, we'll look at how the Direction, or the Path, of Disintegration, will affect you as someone who falls under Personality Type 1. You'll gain a better understanding of the behavioral traits you will take on and how you can identify signs of disintegration early so you can take preventative measures and stave off stress.

Types 1s and Stress

At their best, people with a Type 1 personality type are contentious and pragmatic. They are perfectionists who are constantly trying to do their best and improve as much as possible. They are good at telling right from wrong, are committed to their goals, and work hard to ensure that not only are these goals met but that they are met in the right way.

As a Type 1, you are likely to push your inner feelings aside if doing so will help you handle your responsibilities and complete your tasks. You have a strong internal value system and sense of responsibility, which you use to confirm that you are on the right path.

When you experience stress, you start to become overzealous. You will begin to see things more in black and white and will be unable to recognize the shades of grey and try to suppress your anger. You may also become a workaholic.

If the stress doesn't stop, you'll soon start to display signs of unhealthy 4's. 4's are highly individualistic, and you'll quickly become self-absorbed, self-indulgent, and get lost in fantasies. You may become self-destructive and may even find yourself developing self-loathing and masochistic tendencies.

Disintegrating 1s

1s like to push themselves beyond their limits and often feel like they must be perfect in every aspect of their lives. This is something that can cause significant amounts of internal stress and often lead to disintegration.

It's essential to remember that while you may feel tempted to continue to push yourself, exhaustion can increase the speed at which you disintegrate. As a Type 1, you'll start to feel out of place and misunderstood as you disintegrate. The emotions that you're holding back will begin to creep into your psyche, and you'll find yourself becoming moody and emotional.

You may find yourself connecting emotionally to the arts. While this isn't usually a sign of concern, as a 1, you will become more engaged with art pieces (including music, movies, and books) the more out of place and unsettled you feel. Disintegrating 1s also find themselves pulling away from their loved ones. They will start procrastinating and overthinking things, which will, together, create a vicious cycle of overthinking-procrastination-overthinking, which will only make things worse.

Unhealthy Crutches and Self-Destructive Patterns

As Type 1s disintegrate, they find themselves unable to regulate their emotions as effectively as they once had. This change can be very challenging and can lead 1s to resort to an unhealthy crutch to help them deal with their feelings, such as alcohol or drugs.

At their most extreme, disintegrating 1s can start to exhibit extremely self-destructive patterns, leading them to further lean on their unhealthy crutch to fill the emptiness within themselves.

Procrastination and Overthinking

As Type 1s disintegrate, they start to question everything about themselves. This is in contrast with healthy Type 1s who are confident in their belief system and moral compass. They will begin to question what they have contributed to the world, whether they've achieved enough, and whether their actions have been worth anything.

This pattern of overthinking can lead to 1s being overwhelmed with new emotions that they're not sure how to handle, and they can also start to experience self-doubt. This, in turn, can lead to procrastination and missed deadlines.

Procrastination is especially pronounced in disintegrating 1s if the project they are working on is not creative. While 1s are usually very pragmatic, as they disintegrate into Fours, they'll start to feel more connected to the arts and creativity.

Social Withdrawal

Fours are highly individualistic, and at the negative end, this can lead to social withdrawal. As 1s disintegrate and start to take on negative traits associated with Fours, they'll begin to pull away from the people around them, especially friends and family.

As 1s experience a barrage of negative emotions, they may find themselves depressed and feeling fragile and empty internally. This can cause them to withdraw into themselves, avoiding talking about their emotions as a way to avoid the feelings they are experiencing. They will start to develop self-loathing tendencies and believe that no one will understand their feelings, or they'll be judged negatively for them.

Signs of Disintegration

If you start finding yourself down the Path of Disintegration, the new emotions and negative sensations you're experiencing can leave you shocked and feeling lost. As mentioned above, 1s are particularly susceptible to this, as they will start experiencing all the negative emotions they have worked hard to control as they begin to disintegrate.

To avoid disintegration, it's essential to be able to read the signs and identify what you're experiencing. This will help you take the necessary steps to move off the Path of Disintegration and instead follow the Direction of Integration.

Hypocritical

Unhealthy 1s will be unable to accept criticism of themselves, though they will be quick to give it out. They will pride themselves on being blunt, straight-talkers who "tell it like it is" but will become offended if they are critiqued in turn.

1s under stress will be unable to face their own weakness and will be unwilling to tolerate anything that tries to make them do so. They will see themselves as beyond reproach and critique.

Furthermore, they will often find themselves indulging in activities they may decry publicly. For example, if a 1 promotes the benefits of being a teetotaler, he may be an alcoholic in private. They are unwilling to face the shame that their actions should bring them (based on their internal moral systems) but are comfortable chastising others for similar actions.

Intolerant and Judgmental

Ones in the process of disintegration start to become obsessed with their own values and ideals. They don't have any patience for any diversity of thought and belief and disdain people whose actions waver from their ideals. They are close-minded and domineering and have little patience for anything beyond the poles of black and. They are confident at playing both judge and jury and believe those whose actions differ from their own are corrupt, lazy, incompetent, or evil.

Disintegrating 1s: The Variants

Not all 1s react the same way to going down the Path of Disintegration. While the effects of disintegration are unique for each person, there are three major variants that characterize disintegrating 1s can expect.

The Sexual One

Sexual 1s are on the lookout for a relationship with their ideal significant other, and the relationship is a highly passionate one. However, as they are looking for the ideal partner, they are also looking for a flawless, perfect relationship.

As 1s disintegrate, they will become more critical of their partner and will be controlling and chiding. They are extremely jealous and co-dependent with their other half.

The Social One

Social 1s are those that think of themselves as serving as role models to the people around them. They focus on institutions and work to change them in a positive way.

However, as they disintegrate, they start to see every public policy they disagree with as a personal affront. People who disagree with their beliefs are considered to be attacking them on a personal level.

As they disintegrate, the Social 1s are no longer able to take criticism but get annoyed if people are unwilling to take their own critiques into account or if other people take their critiques personally rather than acting on them. They are hypocritical and judgmental and are intolerant of people with different views.

The Self-Preservation One

Ones who fall into the self-preservation model look to lead an orderly, structured life. They are continuously concerned about their well-being, both in terms of material possessions and health. They are often mistaken for being 6s and often become stressed as they work to ensure their security.

This stress can lead to disintegration, and as they disintegrate, they start to swing between the poles of self-restraint and debauchery. They start to crave giving in to impulses such as binging on alcohol, food, and sex but will react to this by punishing themselves for their desires and restraining from the very practices they crave. At the extreme end of this spectrum, 1s can often end up self-harming or even starving themselves.

What to Do

It's essential to keep an eye on your temperament and learn to identify if you are disintegrating. Some signs of disintegrating 1s include:

- Lack of self-trust

- Procrastination, lack of drive, and ambition

- Envy towards others

- Indignation at unmet expectations and a feeling that you will never achieve your goals

- Isolation and alienation from other people

- Guilt

- Excessive emotion, to the point where it prevents you from meeting your responsibilities

If you start to notice these symptoms in yourself, it's essential to act as soon as possible to prevent further disintegration. Some actions you can take include:

- Recognizing your self-destructive behavior and taking steps to act on it.

- Creating time in their schedules for a break during which you can relax

- Making leisure time for yourself

- Taking the time to identify your internal emotions so that you can express these externally. This can be extremely challenging for someone who falls under personality Type 1. However, doing so will allow you to work out your emotions in a healthy manner rather than internalize them, which can lead to toxic thought patterns.

It's also essential to remember that every person will experience times of stress at some point in their life. Most of us will find ourselves on the Path of Disintegration at least once, and this isn't something that is out of the norm or unusual.

By being able to identify the signs of disintegration, 1s will have a better understanding of how to react when this starts to take place. Additionally, if they have disintegrated in the past, they should be proactive in remembering the experience of disintegration and the negative thought processes that marked it. By doing so, they will be able to prevent themselves from another round of disintegration.

Remember, comfort is never a guarantee in life. However, by understanding how to react to the stressful moments in our lives, we'll be able to adjust how we recover from difficult times. We will also be better able to move down the Direction of Integration rather than the Direction of Disintegration.

Chapter 6: Healthy 1s: The Path of Integration

In the last chapter, we discussed the negative effects that stress can have on a Type 1 personality. We looked at how they can go down the Direction of Disintegration, which ends in their disintegration into a person who displays all of the worst aspects of a Type 4 personality.

However, this is not the only direction that a 1 can travel while going down the movement points. They can also travel down the Direction of Integration and ultimately integrate with the best traits of Type 7.

Type 1s are often known as Perfectionists, and they are driven by a desire to be good and to follow the right path. They value integrity above all and are motivated by their own internal principles.

People of this personality type appreciate structure and standards, and they want to lead by example. They are able to view things objectively without bringing their emotions into a situation, allowing them to be good at judging people.

They are reliable and conscientious and stick to their word, seeing things through to the end. At their best, they are natural leaders and are great at organizing and creating an order. Their critical nature also makes them quality-minded and allows them to see flaws that need to be rectified.

Type 1s are also known as Reformers because they are usually driven by the basic desire to be good and full of integrity. They will work to achieve these "higher values," even if it means significant personal sacrifice.

At the same time, they are also driven by a constant need for justification, both to themselves and to others.

However, Type 1s are not always healthy. They are also driven by the fear of becoming corrupt and evil, and the stress this poses on them can cause them to slip into unhealthy thinking patterns.

At their worst, unhealthy 1s can be judgmental and overly critical. They can be uncompromising and pedantic and find it difficult to accept that others may also have a valid perspective on things if that perspective differs from their own.

1s naturally have difficulty with their emotions, as they push themselves to prevent them from affecting their behavior. However, this repression can lead to 1s with unhealthy thought patterns having problems with aggression and resistance and can become extremely rigid, severe, and unforgiving.

An unhealthy mindset is often the precursor to disintegration and may even river a clue that a person is already traveling down the Direction of Disintegration. In such a situation, it's essential to find a way to the Path of Integration as soon as possible. For 1s, this integration can help them feel more joyful and accepting and significantly reduce their stress as they push themselves to be as perfect as possible.

This chapter will examine the Path of Integration for Type 1s and examine the journey they can take when traveling down this path.

Understanding Integration

As mentioned above, integration is crucial for Type 1s so they can move past the negative traits associated with Type 1. Ones tend to integrate with 7s, which allows them to become freer and, at the same time, rigid.

However, these facts do not answer a basic question you need to have clarity about before you can move down the Path of Integration. What, exactly, is integration anyway?

In the simplest of terms, integration is the other end of the spectrum to disintegration. Where disintegration represents a person slipping into unhealthy thought patterns and becoming the worst version of themselves, integration allows you to become a better person.

Each personality type integrates into another personality type, to which they are linked by one of the Enneagram movement arrows discussed in the previous chapter. The personality type to which you integrate is also known as your growth or security number.

Thus, as a 1, your growth/security number is 7 (the personality type to which you will integrate).

As the name implies, your growth/security number helps you grow as a person. It helps you see the positives in the world around you and allows you to better understand who you are as a person.

Integration and the Levels of Development

As discussed in the previous chapter, the levels of development represent the psyche of a person at any given time. The lower levels (7 to 9) represent the Path of Disintegration, while the average levels (4 to 6) represent a person who is currently secure in their identity and personality type.

The higher levels – levels 1 to 3 – however, represent the path a person will take as they travel up the Path of Integration.

- **Level Three:** The level of social value. It is the level at which we are better able to understand our position in society and start to discern our purpose in life. Ones at this level have truth and justice as their primary values. They have a strong sense of responsibility and personal integrity and are extremely principled. They strive to always be fair and ethical.

- **Level Two:** The level of psychological capacity. At this level, we are able to embrace the hidden aspects of our personalities that we strived to repress, and our personalities become more flexible. Ones at this level have an intense sense of right and wrong and have strong personal and moral values. They are mature, reasonable, and moderate.

- **Level One:** The level of liberation. This is the highest level a person can reach and involves successful integration with their security number. It represents true freedom and is reached when a person has faced and overcome their deepest fears. Ones at this level are able to accept reality as it is. They are hopeful and inspiring and truly believe that the truth will ultimately be heard in every situation, and the right outcome will prevail.

Moving up the levels to reach Level 1 allows people to let go of their unconscious motives and behaviors. They are no longer bound by their core fears and compulsions and are instead able to work toward understanding and harnessing their true power. They are no longer focused on the defensive, unhealthy aspects of their personality type and no longer have to worry about falling victim to harmful thought patterns.

Movement doesn't just represent mental growth – it often represents spiritual and emotional growth as well. As people move up the Levels of Development, they are better able to identify how they are interlinked with the people around them and how their actions affect others (and vice versa). They begin to understand the role they play in the society in which they live, which can help them better understand their role as a whole.

While the Levels of Development represent the way in which you move towards integration, there is another consideration to keep in mind – the Levels of Integration.

These levels examine how deeply you have integrated with your security number. These levels are:

> • **Low:** At this level of integration, you are still bound by the core fears of your personality type. The way you react to your situation corresponds to your Enneagram type, and you cannot access the traits of other personality types (including your security number) as easily as you potentially could. Your capabilities are limited, and you are unable to benefit from the expanded horizons offered by deeper levels of integration.

> • **Moderate:** At the moderate level of integration, you are starting to let go of your core fears – however, you haven't managed to do so completely yet. You're less fixated on issues that caused you to stress previously and are less reactive. However, because you haven't completely let go of your core fears, your actions are still significantly driven by the traits of your personality type. That said, you do have access to other personality types on the Enneagram, including your security number and wings. In some people, this combination of being driven by your personality type but having access to other options can lead to internal conflicts.

> • **High:** At this level, you are essentially fully integrated with your security number. You have finally succeeded in letting go of your personality type's core fears. This allows

you to move toward the center of the Enneagram – when your core type has less of a hold on your actions. Indeed, you are not able to hold on to your core type lightly and fluidly, getting the benefits of its positive traits while also being able to access the traits of other types, including that of your security number.

Like with the Levels of Development, your position on the Levels of Integration is not fixed. You can move up and down the scale depending on the events in your life, the stress you are under, and your personal mindset.

Working towards Integration

It's essential for everyone to keep in mind that moving up the Direction of Integration is a long process, and it will not happen immediately. There are likely to be times during which you will backslide, falling down the Levels of Development – you may even find yourself slipping into the Direction of Disintegration.

However, it's essential to keep going.

As a Type 1, the desire for perfection is embedded in you. If your efforts are not immediately perfect, there is a chance that you may choose to give up or find yourself under significant stress, which is contrary to your goals while traveling the Path of Integration.

As you move up the Path of Integration, it's essential to try and make time for yourself outside of work and achievement goals. You must remind yourself to take the time to enjoy life, rather than simply treating it as a goal that you need to accomplish or a competition you need to win.

You will also need to take the time to understand the source of your stress. As mentioned above, Type 1s are perfectionists – and the root of this desire is often a fear that the people around them will not accept them if they are anything but perfect.

While the rest of the world sees 1s are perfect, they often see themselves as the opposite and cannot bear the thought that other people might have similar thoughts.

1s may not be able to let go of their innate desire for perfectionism. However, by understanding the root of this need, they can stave off the stress that often accompanies this need

As a 1, you need to find a way to see perfection in even the most imperfect situations. The way to do so will differ for everyone. For some people, this can come through external validation. Others may find it beneficial to focus on the small, perfect details in a situation, even when the rest of the scenario seems to be a disaster.

By finding a way to combine your need for perfectionism with the ability to stop yourself from overthinking, you'll find it easier to stay away from the Path of Disintegration.

Additionally, as a 1, you will also need to accept the value of your emotions as you move towards integration. While the ability to keep said emotions at bay can help you remain objective in even the most fraught of situations, repressing your emotions for too long can create a pressure-keg and often leads to 1s "exploding" when the stress gets too much.

It's essential to find a healthy outlet for your emotions. If you work in a field where objectivity is essential, look for spaces in which you can work out your aggression without affecting that. This can include physical sports, martial arts training, or even having a friend or relative to vent with. By accepting and working through your emotions, you'll soon find that you're happier both emotionally and mentally than you were before and that moving up the Path of Integration is suddenly easier than you may have thought it to be.

Type 1 in Integration

As 1s integrate, they adopt the positive attributes of 7s. 7s are also known as the Enthusiasts or the Epicures. Their basic desire is the desire to be satisfied and content, and by adopting some of their positive characteristics, 1s can find themselves letting go of their repression.

As 1s move toward integrating with 7s, they are more able to pay attention to the good in the world. They become far less critical – of themselves and of others – and are better able to accept themselves as they themselves are.

Integrating and integrated 1s find it easier to be enthusiastic and optimistic and have a much better hold on their emotions. Their feelings are far less internal, and they find it easier to share this part of who they are with the people they love. They will also find that their inner critic is less outspoken and more able to enjoy each moment of life as it takes place.

1s in integration find it easier to accept the positives in life, and they are far more joyful and accepting than they were. They can also find themselves feeling refreshed and grounded and acting more naturally and spontaneously. At their best, integrated 1s will find it easier to play activities for enjoyment rather than as a means to an end.

In integration, you will also find yourself feeling more creative than you ever have and far more confident and secure in yourself. They will be more curious and able to rebound from setbacks easier than when they were ruled solely by personality Type 1.

However, 1s should keep in mind that integration takes time and effort. Many 1s find it challenging to express themselves during integration, as they are more focused on the tasks that they "should" be doing instead. If you feel yourself slipping into these thought patterns, look for something to distract you so that you don't slip back down the Levels of Development.

Things to Expect During Integration

As discussed above, 1s in integration need to learn to relax and take some time for themselves without stressing out about doing so.

It's also essential to remember that no one can change immediately. This is not only true for you, but it's also true for other people. By understanding that people take time to change, you'll become a better teacher and leader and develop patience.

At the same time, be careful not to get annoyed at what you see as other people's shortcomings. If you're able to pause and take in all sides of a situation, you'll often find your perspective expanded, and you'll be able to recognize that just because people don't act exactly as you would, it doesn't mean that they aren't right in their own way. Taking the time to pause and consider all the factors will help you become more flexible and accepting of other people and less stringent when it comes to your own thought patterns.

As discussed above, as a 1, you need to get in touch with the emotions you may have repressed. At the same time, it's also essential to recognize the anger that you've been repressing using more positive emotions serves as your Achilles heel.

1s get angry easily, especially when the structure they have created in their minds is not being adhered to. As you open yourself up to the emotions that you have repressed, you need to work through these emotions, including the anger.

However, moving past is not necessarily the road you'll have to take for all your emotions. Many other desires, including sexual and aggressive impulses, need to be faced head-on. These are the messy parts of life that make you human, and dealing with them will make it easier for you to let go of your control and accept the moments in life as they come to you.

The Relationship between 1s and 7s

As mentioned above, integration is not always smooth sailing. It requires work and effort. This is especially true for 1s, as they will be integrating with a personality type that is significantly different from their own.

Whereas 1s are organized and often map out their every action, 7s are far more spontaneous and relaxed. Unlike 7s, 1s are driven by a desire for justice, morality, and "goodness" rather than a desire for self-fulfillment and satisfaction.

While these types can seem to be at opposite ends of the personality spectrum, being able to integrate your Type 1 personality with Type 7 allows you to become far more balanced as an individual. Being able to focus on yourself as well as the world around you will prevent you from burning out in the way that many others 1s do, and your desire for the order will allow you to control the more whimsical nature of 7s.

Type 1 of your personality can help you identify long-term opportunities and commit to them, while the integrated 7 will help you be more flexible, artistic, and creative, and relaxed.

Additionally, through integration, you will find it easier to deal with change. Ones often find change difficult to navigate because they prefer the order of the known, but the integrated 7 will help you adapt to your new circumstances and see the positives in the change you are experiencing.

As someone who falls under personality Type 1, you are motivated by a desire for social change, helping others, finding effective (and "right") solutions to problems, and growing as a person.

Sevens, on the other hand, are more creative and are motivated by the desire for new experiences and ideas, getting to know new people, and having greater creativity.

By integrating these aspects, you bolster both halves of your personality. The integrated 7 will help you come up with creative, unique, and effective solutions to the challenges you have been working on. At the same time, the 1 will make it easier for the 7 in your personality to work within yourself in order to help you to grow as a person, rather than focusing on the rest of the world.

As you go through the integration process, you'll see that there's more to you than even you would have thought possible, and you'll figure out what steps you need to take to become the best version of yourself you can be.

Chapter 7: Type 1 Wing 9 — The Idealist

In this chapter, we will be discussing the Type 1 Wing 9 personality types, also referred to as the Idealists. But, before we jump into learning more about this personality type, you must be wondering, "What does Wing even mean?" Wing refers to the subtype that goes with the main or dominant type. For example, being a Type 1 with Wing 9 means that these individuals mainly possess qualities of Type 1 but also have a few qualities of a Type 9 personality. It is important to note that you can have more than one wing. Usually, personality types have more than one wing, and they can affect the overall personality of the individual.

The proportion of the wing score must always be considered when studying a personality type. This can tell us more about the individual's personality. This includes how they think and perceive things, what their fears and motivations are, and how they function in their daily lives. Studying personality types with their wings can also help you better understand what kind of childhood you must have had and how to tend to the emotional wounds of your childhood.

However, you must always consider the possibility of getting a different wing than our true personality types as your current life situation can seriously affect it.

Type 1 wing 9 individuals are usually rational, calm, and balanced personalities with a strong sense of right and wrong. These personalities seek to bring justice to all parties and are great at mediating between different parties as they can weigh up both sides of a problem easily. This helps them come to a just conclusion where both parties feel justified. These personality types like to keep to themselves and rarely let their emotions come to the surface. Let's dive into their childhood to learn what led to the formation of these personalities.

Childhood

Our childhood has a significant effect on our lives as it shapes who we grow up to be. Our relationships with our parents and our caretakers affect our future relationships with our friends, families, and potential partners. Even though our personality type remains the same throughout our lives, we can work toward unlearning our unhealthy traits and developing our positive traits to become healthier versions of our personalities.

During their childhood years, Type 1 individuals may have had a disconnected relationship with their parents. Moreover, it is also possible that their caretakers were either too strict or too lenient. This could also mean that the parent they wanted to lean on for protection was abusive or arbitrary and distracted, and so, they always felt the need to please them and never make them angry. If these children grow up in extremely religious households, they may also develop a need to please an angry God who is easily angered and must be feared. Having a dysfunctional relationship with the parental or protective figure can lead these personalities to maintain a strict set of boundaries for themselves so that no one can question them. This is why they often grow up as individuals who appear to have strict morals and ethics. Their need to maintain a spotless reputation stems from their experiences in childhood.

These children had to stay vigilant all the time to avoid criticism or making their parents angry. They are extremely sensitive to criticism. They always feel the need to keep things in control to keep everyone from getting angry. It is possible that these children were never allowed to act like children and were always expected to act like adults. Due to this, they internalize the role of the punishing father and grow up maintaining a strict code of ethics for themselves. However, there is a possibility that these children have had a good childhood but want to achieve better things in life.

Due to their childhood, these children try to become their own caretakers and develop a strict set of rules for themselves. They implement these rules on themselves to bring some structure and discipline into their lives that were never offered by their primary parents or guardians. This is why they try their best to control their feelings and emotions. However, when they see others who do not have control over their feelings, they feel angry and blame themselves for it.

This behavior stems from always being at the end of their angry parent's pointing finger. The fear of being criticized or blamed can become quite overwhelming, and why they're always striving for perfection at the expense of enjoying childhood. On the other hand, these children have the ability to grow up to work on their negative traits to become the healthiest versions of themselves. They can learn to think rationally and not hold themselves accountable for every little thing that goes wrong. They are also more tolerant and accepting of others.

Workplace

People with Type 1 Wing 9 tend to have more qualities of their Type 1 (reformer). These individuals are perfectionists and are extremely cautious, and are frightened to make mistakes. They want to maintain their spotless reputation. This is why these personalities tend to thrive in environments where all expectations and communications are clear. Such people tend to excel at careers in the educational sector, police departments, and judicial sectors. As a Type 1 Wing 9, you are detail-oriented and tend to do well in jobs that require you to dissect and analyze situations and look for loopholes. This is why Type 1s tend to do great in careers as detectives, lawyers, or architects. Type 1s have a strong sense of right and wrong. They like to seek justice and help the powerless. This is why they also strive in careers like being social workers, counselors, and attorneys. Enneagram-Type 1s with Wing 9 are diplomatic and diligent individuals. They do well in environments where they feel encouraged and accepted. They do great in an environment that is not overly critical.

Here are a few careers that are great for Type 1s Wing 9:

- Judge
- Social Worker
- Environmentalist
- Guidance Counselor
- Journalist
- Public Relations Specialist
- Consultant
- Ambassador

Type 1s are averse to criticism from others, especially when it's meant to be harsh. Moreover, you don't want to be perceived as weak, which is why you must never opt for careers in hospitality or customer services which may expose you to harsh criticism or put you in a position where you're presumed to be weak. Additionally, you do not want to work in a job where you feel that you're not making a difference. You also don't want to be humiliated or ignored. Being recognized for the work that you do means a lot to the idealist in you. You also don't tend to be good at careers where you're expected to be involved in corruption, injustice, or other evil acts.

When in the wrong environment, Type 1s can become non-adaptable. These people should avoid being in environments where their ideas are ignored or where they are made to feel out of control. They should also avoid being in roles where making mistakes is inevitable. These personalities require instructions to work, and they should avoid places where they are not given clear instructions. Moreover, Type 1s should also avoid becoming accountants as they tend to become extremely anal and compulsive.

Here are the careers that are the absolute worst for Type 1s:

- Management Assistant
- Representatives of Retail
- Auditors
- Customer Services

Strengths of Type 1w9

Type 1s are rational and reasonable people. They operate on logic and clear goals. This makes them great team players as they're able to see through every situation while working towards a common goal with their teammates. As these personalities are quite principled, they always believe in doing the right thing for everyone. This quality makes them trustworthy and reliable people to have around. Ones have a strict code of ethics, which is why everyone trusts their ability to make decisions.

Type 1 wing 9 are purposeful individuals. This makes them cautious individuals who will never do anything impulsive that could potentially harm someone. Due to their honest, responsible, and positive attitude, these individuals are trusted by the majority, and everyone trusts them for their ability to work for the common good.

Healthy Ones make for amazing and loyal friends who are always there for everyone. They put their friends first and are reliable and trustworthy people. These healthy versions of Type 1 personalities are not overly critical of themselves and allow themselves to make mistakes. They don't hold themselves to high levels and give themselves the liberty to be wrong. At their best, the Type 1s with Wing 9 are great people, gifted writers, and powerful orators. They are extremely talented when it comes to writing and speaking and using any medium of communication.

- These people are extremely detail-oriented
- They are honest
- They are very responsible individuals
- They are rational and reasonable humans
- These people are improvement-oriented
  - They make extremely talented writers and speakers
  - Loyal friends
  - Very thoughtful and kind
  - Stand up for the powerless and underprivileged
  - They have an optimistic and imaginative world-view
  - Work towards the common good of the society
  - They are compassionate individuals
  - They have a strong code of ethics

Weakness of Type 1Wing 9

Unhealthy Type 1s Wing 9 tend to repress their emotions and feelings. This can lead them to explode after a while. Other than that, due to their repressed feelings, they move around with a certain rigidity that shows up in the form of nervous gestures or tics.

These people can also become quite anxious in situations where they're not in control. Moreover, they can become extremely self-critical and question their memory to the point of gaslighting themselves. This makes these people extremely compulsive, leading them to repeat behaviors again and again. Being perfectionists, these Types have a strong tendency to become extremely anal. Their over-critical nature can cause them to get stuck in their head, due to which they may come off as reserved, dry, and quiet.

- Need to be in control of everything.
- Tendency to become compulsive
- Can be rigid
- Can become non-adaptable in the worst environments
- Tend to find faults in others
- Can become self-critical.
- Stubborn
- Tend to repress their feelings
- Can be extremely sensitive to criticism

Desires of Type 1w9

The basic desire of Type 1s Wing 9 is just to be a morally responsible individual who can make a positive impact on the world. They want to be involved in projects where they feel like their work is making a difference. They want to stand up for the powerless and have the need to do right by everyone. They want to be the best versions of themselves and want to be in control of their surroundings. Moreover, their innermost deep desire is to grow and evolve and learn from their mistakes to never make them again.

In short:

- Make a difference in the world
- To do right by everyone
- To be just and act justly
- Helping the powerless
- Analyzing and solving complex issues
- Personal and professional development and growth

Fears of Type 1w9

The biggest fear of these individuals is to become unethical or corrupt, always wanting to make the right choices and never do wrong by anyone. Moreover, they also fear getting a bad reputation. Hence, they try their best to keep their record clean and avoid making any mistakes by often falling into a mechanical lifestyle. As perfectionists, they also fear displeasing others and getting harsh criticism.

They are sensitive to harsh criticism and fear being criticized

They fear being ignored

They fear making the wrong choice

They fear becoming corrupt or unethical

They have a fear of making unredeemable mistakes

Type 1s are logical, rational, and responsible individuals. You are an idealist because you see the best in people and want to do your best for them. However, often due to your dysfunctional childhood and estranged parent figures, you may feel disconnected from other people. Type 1 Wing 9 may have to deal with an inner conflict as

Type 1 needs to bring about change to the world or "reform," whereas Type 9s do not like change. They have trouble coming out of their comfort zones. This can cause a conflict within Type 1s with Wing 9s. These individuals are also extremely cautious. This makes them take a step back from their surroundings and evaluate the situations rationally.

Healthier Ones are reasonable people with sound judgment and logical thinking. They tend to be at peace with others and themselves. They do not hold themselves accountable for everything that goes wrong. Moreover, the healthier Ones make for great friends who are always there for everyone. As adults, they can turn out to be wonderful orators, gifted writers, and educated individuals with a strong code of discipline and ethics. These people are wary of the evil in the world and any sort of corruption that plagues the world. They want to bring justice to the powerless and have a strong desire to make a difference in the world. However, they do tend to be stiff and inflexible when it comes to dealing with criticism. Overall, the Type 1s with a 9 Wing make wonderful and loyal friends who are compassionate and just want to do right by everyone.

Chapter 8: Type 1 Wing 2 — The Activist

In the last chapter, we analyzed the pairing of Type 1 with the subtype 9, the idealist. In this chapter, we will take a look at the pairing of type 1 with subtype 2, the activist. Although the main type of these individuals is the same, their subtypes can have a significant effect on their overall personalities. Type 1s are loyal and humble individuals that find joy in serving others. These individuals believe in working hard towards a better tomorrow while keeping their integrity and morals intact. Type 1s make wonderful, cautious leaders that think critically before taking any step. They are always working to become their best selves and hence, greatly believe in self-development and growth. As we discussed in the previous chapter, the type 1w9 are rational and reasonable individuals whose main purpose in life is to make a difference in the world and create a significant impact in everything they do. We also learned how these individuals don't let their emotions come to the surface easily, which leads to them acting fidgety and nervous.

Let's take a look at the similarities and differences between the healthy/unhealthy type 1w9 and type 1w2.

Healthy 1w9 vs. Healthy 1w2

Healthy 1w9 personalities can look at the world through a precise but imaginary worldview. They can look at the big picture of things while also considering all the factors of the situation. These personalities try their best to keep peace among their surroundings. This quality stems from their "peacemaker" subtype, Type 9. However, healthy 1w9s allow themselves to make mistakes and don't hold themselves to super-human standards. They don't hold themselves accountable for things that are not in their control. These people are also believed to be extremely talented when it comes to speaking or writing.

On the other hand, healthy Types 1w2 are more in touch with their feelings and emotions. Unlike 1w9s, they are more attuned to their emotions and do not repress their feelings as 1w9s do. They allow themselves to feel the so-called negative feelings like anger or sadness. Because they can feel emotions and be at peace, they are also able to make other people feel better. They are extremely compassionate and helpful individuals; this is why they want to create solutions for other people. They are caring individuals who are always there for their close ones. They have a great ability to care for others without making them feel suffocated. Moreover, contradictory to 1w9s, they like to connect with other people on a deeper level. These individuals also tend to focus more on the acts of self-love and self-care.

Unhealthy 1w9 VS. Unhealthy 1w2

In unfavorable circumstances, 1w9s become closed off and detach themselves from their surroundings. This is their way of dissociating themselves and an unhealthy coping mechanism to deal with their negative thoughts and emotions. They tend to indulge in binge-watching and binge-eating - unhealthy things to avoid reality. When 1w9s feel out of control, they find faults in other people and how they are not doing anything right. They may isolate themselves to make sense of their feelings and things around them. Unhealthy 1w9s also can become extremely self-critical. They can become obsessed with everything they're doing wrong and may put themselves to impossibly high standards.

Unhealthy 1w2s can become extremely bossy, and they feel like they need to take charge of every situation because they feel they are the only people who know the right thing to do. This stems from their perception of themselves as the "savior." This can make their close friends and family feel suffocated. If they are not allowed to do things in their way, they may become whiny and may rant about how they are always treated badly. In their low periods, they may drown in self-pity. These individuals are quite vocal with their disapproval, which often escalates the situation making things worse between them and their loved ones. This is not the enneagram 1.

Childhood

As has been said, our personalities are formulated in childhood. Our relationships with our parents, siblings, and any other authoritative person in charge shape the person we are today. A person retains their core personality traits throughout their life. However, in different circumstances, they may act differently.

Type 1s usually have a restrained relationship with their parents. Because of insecure childhoods, these little people felt the need to discipline themselves. This may have led them to create strict boundaries. On the other hand, it is also possible that they unconsciously internalized the behavior of their extremely strict parents. Due to the unfair treatment by their parents, these children often felt alone and isolated, especially when the abuse was coming from the one person who was supposed to protect them. This creates an inherent need in them to save the powerless and shield those who cannot protect themselves.

Moreover, as they could not confide in their parents and might be punished for showing emotions (sadness or anger), they repressed their emotions. This is why they grow up to become detached individuals who seem to have trouble connecting with others. In their low moments, these individuals become detached to protect themselves from negative thoughts and situations. Because of their background, they become perfectionists. This causes them to grow up with a strict code of ethics and morals. They hold themselves accountable for making any mistakes or violating their own boundaries due to the internalized behavior of their parents.

However, they can learn to unlearn their unhealthy patterns and way of thinking. Healthy 1w2s that have grown out of their unhealthy traits are principled, compassionate, logical, and ethical people who genuinely want the good for people. These individuals are warm and care for others with a genuine concern for their problems and difficulties. They try to act like their own worst critics so that no one else can blame them. They justify their existence by helping others and living a disciplined life. However, healthier 1w2s believe that they need as much love and care as others do. This is why they frequently indulge in self-care and self-loving behaviors.

Workplace

These types do well in careers where they are able to serve others. They like to know that they have a positive impact on others and are of some use. Type 1w2s love to be in leadership positions where they are able to organize and manage people. When unhealthy, these individuals can become extremely bossy, and this may lead them to micromanage others. When healthy, they like to be a mentor and a friend to their subordinates. They are great at taking charge of situations and taking control when there's a need. These people do well under pressure and in difficult situations. However, they don't feel strongly about giving the other person control and can find it difficult when a more dominant person shows up.

Type1w2s are driven by the sense of right and wrong. They are selfless, action-oriented, rational, compassionate, and thoughtful. They feel it's their duty to educate and help others. This is how they justify their existence on this planet. They love to care for others, and this is why they are often doctors, nurses, judges, and social workers, etc. You will find them involved in public causes and services to others. These people allow themselves to feel and express themselves emotionally while also maintaining control over themselves. This helps them do better at sensitive professions like that of nurses and doctors.

These people make great:

- Nurses
- Judges
- Politicians
- Doctors
- Lawyers
- Social Advocates
- Real Estate Agents
- Social Workers
- Religious Workers

These personalities don't do well in environments where they are criticized and not appreciated. They don't want to be made to feel like they are useless. These individuals thrive on caring for others. This is why they don't want to be made to feel like they are not meeting the needs of others and are not useful to the people around them. They do not like to disappoint others. This is why they should avoid careers where making mistakes is inevitable. They should never get into careers where they won't feel appreciated or where they are unable to serve other people.

These are the careers type 1w2 should avoid:

- Accountants

- Retail Representatives

- Administrative Assistants

Strengths of Type 1w2

Type 1w2 individuals like to be in service to others. These are extremely kind, thoughtful, and compassionate human beings who genuinely have a love for their fellow humans and other creatures in this world. These people are sensitive to the needs of others and have a heart of gold. Due to their great interpersonal skills, they can solve difficult problems, including the issues pertinent to society. They have a great capability to be organized, methodical, and improvement-oriented. Due to their ability to deeply care for others, they make up to be great friends who are always there for the people close to them.

Some of the greatest strengths of the Type 1w2 are:

- They always stand for what's right.

- They fight for the rights of those who can't defend themselves.

- They are sensitive to the needs of the people around them.

- They have a genuine love for humanity.

- They find joy in serving humanity.

- They have the tremendous ability to take control over difficult situations.

- They make up to be amazing friends.

- They do the right thing (even if it's a hard thing to do!)

- They are extremely wise individuals.

- They make up wonderful mentors.

- These people are usually fun and energetic individuals.

Weakness of Type 1w2

The 1w2 personalities are usually perfectionists. They feel that their way is the best way. When someone disagrees with their way of doing things, they get angry. They will also make sure that the other person knows about their disapproval by whining and complaining loudly. These people don't want to be criticized by others for their ideals. However, when someone does criticize them, they may guilt-trip them for doing so. They also tend to feel righteous for completely self-serving acts. When stressed, the 1w2 types may go against their ideals and indulge in drugs, sex, and alcohol. Moreover, they may even act passive-aggressive when in a fight.

- These individuals are extremely harsh on themselves.

- They see things in black and white.

- They do not like to deal with sudden changes in plans.

- They might become manipulative and self-serving.

- At their worst, they may violate their ideals.

Desires of Type 1w2

The underdog and the powerless people whose rights have been infringed will have this Type2w2 rushing in to help. This is why you will often find them involved in social causes. They also feel the need to be in control of their emotions and their surroundings. They need to mentor those around them and help them become the best versions of themselves.

- They have a strong desire to help the powerless.

- They want to be in control of their situation.

- They want to have self-control.

- They want to make a positive impact on this world.

Fears of Type 1w2

The basic fear of Type 1w2 is to be criticized for their beliefs and ideals. They don't want to feel belittled or like they are not needed. They also fear not being enough for those they love. They genuinely want to offer love and care to the people close to them. This is why they fear disappointing them or feeling like they are not fulfilling their expectations. They also have a deep fear of going against their ethical values.

- These people fear violating their boundaries.

- These individuals fear disappointing their loved ones. This isn't the enneagram 1.

- They fear not being needed.

- They fear being criticized for their ideals.

Type 1w2s predominantly possess the Type 1 traits, with some elements of their subtype 2, which make them warm, kind, compassionate, thoughtful, rational, and reasonable. The healthy versions of this type love to be there for others. They have a great desire to help the powerless. You will often find these people fighting for the underdog. During their childhoods, these people may have had a restrained relationship with their parents, and it is possible they had abusive parents and had to act like adults. The lack of protection and warmth in their childhood leads them to become protective of powerless and underprivileged people in society. Contrary to type 1w9, they don't need to suppress their emotions and feelings. They allow themselves to feel while retaining self-control. The healthier versions of these personalities can practice self-love and self-care. However, in stressful situations, these people can become manipulative and self-serving. They feel like they are righteous when the reality may be different. However, when healthy, these people make out to be caring and lovely individuals.

The 1w2 personalities do well at jobs that revolve around serving others. This is why they make wonderful social workers, doctors, nurses, and judges, etc. They have a strong desire to make a positive impact on the world while keeping their ethical values intact. However, they fear criticism and may become defensive when their ideas are questioned. Moreover, they become their worst versions when they feel like they are not needed. They also tend to become bossy and controlling and may get offended when they're told that their help is not needed. However, these people find genuine joy in helping others and have genuine concerns and love for the people around them. They act with their heart and live to serve humanity.

Chapter 9: Relationships with Other Types

Now that we have established your personality traits as the Perfectionist, it's time to talk about how you interact with other types. Every type is unique and has different desires and motivations. Matching two types together can lead to a harmonious relationship depending on their ability to respect each other's differences. In this chapter, we'll explain the compatibility between Type 1s and other types in the Enneagram spectrum in romantic, friendly, and professional relationships.

The Perfectionist with the Perfectionist

As Perfectionists, both of you are pragmatic and always aim to better yourselves in the workplace. You're both familiar with hard work and welcome any challenges that come your way. However, your approach to solving issues can be different, and that's when trouble starts to arise. For optimum results, you can divide tasks and assignments so that each person is responsible for a specific project. Contradictions are easier to resolve in the workplace because there's usually no room for suppressed emotions that can happen in other relationships.

This match also makes for a great friendship. You're both loyal, responsible, and aware of each other's needs. Perfectionists appreciate clear communication, which can sometimes be perceived as bluntness by other types. You both give each other your personal space and know when and how to give advice. As a Type 1, you do not like criticism from others because you tend to be hard on yourself as you beat yourself up for the slightest mistakes. That's why another Perfectionist is the best person who can be there for you when you're stuck on an issue and can give you a fresh perspective.

When it comes to a romantic relationship, it can get a bit tricky. Let's look at the positive side. When in tune with your Type 1 partner, you both strive to bring the best out of each other. You share life responsibilities equally in terms of taking care of your children, doing chores, or setting a monthly budget. You inspire each other to do the best at work and home and respect each other's boundaries.

On the downside, you both tend to suppress your emotions as you take time to analyze and deal with them. This leads to unintentional passive-aggressive behavior, which comes out in the form of sarcastic comments and excessive bickering. You express your criticism towards your partner the same way you do with yourself, which can be destructive in a relationship. To overcome this, make an effort to express your feelings as soon as you can to avoid building them up. Plan a weekly date with your partner when you can discuss any issues in your relationship. This regular practice will get you in the habit of expressing your emotions in a healthy way, which is very helpful in your relationship.

The Perfectionist with the Helper

The Helper or Type 2 personality is concerned with contributing to the wellness of other people. They notice the needs of others and work hard to try to fulfill them. In the process, Helpers usually forget their own needs because they only feel useful when serving others. In many ways, the Perfectionist and the Helper personality types complement each other.

In your careers, both of you work hard as you have a strong sense of duty and responsibility. Even though your methodologies are different, you can find yourselves in similar roles professionally like teaching, medicine, law, politics, and journalism. Your perfectionist nature makes you want to constantly change yourself for the better, which is why you work so hard. On the other hand, the Helper goes above and beyond to help others, so it's not about being better personally but being present at all times to look after other people. Working together can be beneficial as you both tend to throw yourselves at work to achieve the best outcomes.

As friends, Perfectionists and Helpers make a good match. Your Type 2 friend will help you get out of your work mode and relax. They remind you that there are other aspects of life that are less stressful. Helpers are good listeners as they are nurturers and know how to handle other people's feelings. This is one of the qualities that attract you to a friend with a Type 2 personality since they don't necessarily give you advice but help you get your emotions out.

A relationship between Types 1 and 2 makes sense in many aspects. You both display high levels of maturity and independence and can compartmentalize your emotions with your social groups. A sense of achievement means a lot to you both, and you can get that at work or when helping others without putting a strain on your relationship.

Sometimes, this compartmentalization of emotions can create a distance in your relationship. Every once in a while, you'll feel you need some attention from your Helper partner and become jealous of how they always focus on others rather than on your relationship. If you don't express your needs clearly with your partner, this might become an issue. Try not to be critical of their tendency to serve others because that comes as first nature to them. Instead, communicate your concerns genuinely with your partner, as the Helper type will appreciate your honesty.

The Perfectionist with the Achiever

The Achiever shares your values and discipline in the workplace. They are goal-oriented and work hard to meet their objectives. Type 3 sets high and sometimes impossible standards for themselves, which matches your Perfectionist nature. You both cherish practicality and know-how to set aside any emotions which could interfere with your work, making you excellent business partners.

Since you're both workaholics, you will most likely develop a nice friendship. You enjoy working on projects together as you understand each other perfectly. You support one another during the day and have fun in the evening as you both adopt the work-hard-play-hard motto. You don't care for arguments or backbiting, and you support each other in your time of need. All these traits will nurture a lifelong friendship.

This combination can make a successful couple. You both strive for excellence and work hard to accomplish your goals. You love to share life's responsibilities together and make plans for the future. You're both energetic and boost each other's confidence all the time, which is key to a successful partnership which all goes to show how much you respect each other's individuality and boundaries as you both feel proud and privileged to share your life together.

This kind of relationship may sometimes suffer if jealousy creeps in. If one of you is more accomplished than the other, the other one might feel left out. As a Perfectionist, you may sometimes question your partner's ethical standards, which can break the rules. Type 3s can sometimes lose perspective of their principles and want to achieve their goals no matter the cost. On the other hand, if they feel you're too critical of their choices, it could lead them to drift from your relationship. Unfortunately, breakups are common in this particular pairing.

The Perfectionist with the Individualist

Individualists are all about creativity, art, and beauty. They work hard to bring beauty to everything they do. Unlike Perfectionists, Type 4s know exactly how to express their feelings, which complements your personality so well. Working together, you bring your efficiency and pragmatism, and they bring their unique vision to the project. Their artistic nature is inspirational to you, which feeds your need to perfect your job. You help them organize their work and bring everything into focus as they tend to drift away with their imagination.

The Individualist tends to come to you for advice when they feel overwhelmed. Usually, their emotions are all over the place, and they know that you'll give them an honest opinion. On the opposite side, you'll reach out to your Type 4 friend when you can't express your emotions. If you're having a romantic issue or getting mixed signals from your love interest, Type 4 will help you figure out your feelings and give you advice on how to approach your crush.

In romance, your opposite natures come together beautifully. You help ground your partner and bring them back to reality, and they show you how to stop and smell the roses. You're attracted to the Individualist's sensitivity and vulnerability because you feel needed. They show you how to be kind to yourself and stop the constant self-criticism.

Trouble occurs when you don't try to blend in with each other's traits. You'll start to notice your differences as you criticize their lack of discipline and practicality. Type 4s won't be able to handle your judgments on their life choices, and this is when everything can fall apart. You can both wear each other out with never-ending arguments. It helps to give each other some space to calm down when things get heated and then re-visit the subject later.

The Perfectionist with the Investigator

Type 1s and 5s have many similar personality traits, especially when it comes to expressing emotions. You both work with logic and facts as you appreciate clarity and honesty. This helps you work together in perfect coordination as you both enjoy having intellectual debates. You share philosophies about life and culture with a witty sense of humor.

Investigators and Perfectionists make good friends as you find yourselves sharing many interests. Type 5s are often curious about the world, and they spend their time trying to understand how it works. They usually like alone time to pursue their interests, which you appreciate and respect. Since neither of you is expressive, you show your appreciation through acts of service or favors. Your shared pragmatism is what fosters a harmonious, lifelong friendship.

In a relationship, you can thrive together as you establish a foundation of respect. You're far from any relationship drama that can happen with other types. You appreciate each other's differences and learn from them. You benefit from the Investigator's analytical nature and usually ask them for their insights. As a Type 1, you like to follow or set rules as you seek justice in everything you do. Your partner can help you broaden your horizons and see matters from a different perspective.

Your conflicts arise when your partner offers you a lot of gray areas in discussions. To them, things are never in black and white; basically, they don't believe in specific frames or rules. They may start to see you as rigid with your unswerving convictions. Conflict causes Type 5s to drift apart and become even less expressive. This can create a distant relationship, and you may lose touch with what attracted you to each other in the first place.

The Perfectionist with the Loyalist

These two personality types share many good qualities that can make any relationship thrive. As a Type 1, you bring your sense of commitment to the table, which Type 6 appreciates as they yearn for stability. When it comes to working, you both display seriousness, hard work, and integrity. You tend to take the leadership role as you're more decisive than Type 6. Loyalists usually doubt themselves and look up to you for advice, which you gladly give as you appreciate their admiration. They shine in areas that deal with people as they're more approachable.

Your friendship with Type 6 is a long-lasting one. Loyalists are fun to be around as they have a good sense of humor and love to play around. They can be somewhat pessimistic, and you play an important role in making them feel better about themselves.

In relationships, you appreciate the warmth and emotional availability of Type 6. They give a lot in a relationship and show you how to have a good time, which you sometimes desperately need. You have no problems sharing life's responsibilities with the Loyalists as you're both committed to one another.

If you put too much pressure on yourself at work, you can be too hard on yourself and your partner. You tend to overexert yourself, and that can become overwhelming to a Type 6. Before you know it, you'll be arguing more and more every day, and your emotional distance can make your partner insecure. You have to remember to take a step back and make yourself more emotionally available to your partner.

The Perfectionist with the Enthusiast

Type 7 loves adventure and trying new things. As a Perfectionist, you find these traits exciting and refreshing. At work, the Enthusiast is energetic and full of ideas, which makes them a great asset in brainstorming sessions. You appreciate their contribution and help them organize their thoughts. You're more attentive to detail and help them to focus when they drift away from the given topic. The Enthusiast at the workplace makes you feel that there's no problem they can't overcome. This helps you to be more flexible and optimistic.

Type 7s know how to get you out of your comfort zone. They encourage you to go on crazy trips and try different activities. You'll need a Type 7 when you take a break from work, as they know how to have fun. Enthusiasts love your reliability and pragmatism when they have difficulty making decisions, so they often come to you for advice.

As a couple, you fill the gaps in each other's personalities. You apply your firmness and practicality in making life decisions, and they instill a sense of enjoyment and liveliness in your relationship. They encourage you to take chances in life as you sometimes can get stuck in a routine. Together, you balance each other out as you embark upon new adventures and projects.

On the downside, focusing too much on practicality and never stopping to take a breath can take its toll on your relationship. Enthusiasts love to experience life to the fullest, and if you prioritize work too much, they get irritated with your overachieving behavior. Sometimes, you need to let go of life's responsibilities and enjoy your time with your partner.

The Perfectionist with the Challenger

While you share many qualities with the Challenger, you need to be careful how you present yourself. You both crave leadership and being in control, and sometimes, that can be contradicting, especially in the workplace. If you learn how to accept each other's strong opinions, you will be able to work together as you both have a lot to offer. You know how to manage projects, and you can experience a solid partnership at work.

Your Type 8 friend likes to be free and independent. They appreciate people who respect their boundaries, which comes as first nature to you. You're a reliable friend to the Challenger, and they sometimes need someone they can trust with their emotions. It takes time to build trust with a Challenger before they can open up to you. They appreciate your straightforwardness as they resent passive-aggressive behavior, and you know to give them their space when they get angry.

In a relationship, you can make a power couple that works toward a common goal. You share values of justice and public service. You both have a great sense of purpose and share a passion for making things right. Type 8 is more confrontational and challenging, which you find exciting as you tend to hold back. You are attracted to the undeniable presence of the Challenger and appreciate how they take charge.

Due to your different approaches, miscommunication can occur. A Challenger can be like an unstoppable train. They keep going until they achieve their purpose, and then they set out to find another one. You quickly start to see the defaults of the Challenger's personality and criticize them. They start to feel suffocated in your relationship, which causes them to back out or provoke you even more. Without setting some ground rules, this relationship can lead to chaos, and you'll end up resenting the qualities you were attracted to in the first place.

The Perfectionist with the Peacemaker

Peacemakers provide harmony in their relationships. They're more laid back than you, and they rarely clash with your opinions. At work, you're both self-sacrificing and like to work for the greater good, as you share interests in public service. You know how to set aside your differences, if any, to achieve your work goals. The Peacemaker's flexibility helps make them excellent co-workers in a big project.

You appreciate your Type 9 friend because they know when to give you space and when to support you. They're excellent listeners and very diplomatic, so they'll sound their opinions with zero criticism. You encourage them to speak up more and pursue their passions because they tend to lack decisiveness. Make a habit of expressing your gratitude to them for being supportive, as they can get insecure if you're distant.

In romance, Type 9 is easy-going and non-confrontational, which helps keep you calm. You tend to exert too much effort at work, and your partner knows how to absorb your stress and help you relax. You always try to lift your partner's spirit and encourage them to achieve more. They find you inspirational as you help them to explore their true potential.

However, once your criticizing streak begins, the Peacemaker gradually withdraws from your relationship. They don't like confrontation as they try to avoid conflict at all costs. Unfortunately, this causes you to perceive your partner as weak and start to withdraw as well. If you want to salvage this relationship, you need to understand your partner's nature as it's opposite from yours.

The level of maturity is a crucial indicator of the success of any relationship. This means that any type can get along with other types despite their differences. People need to give each other the space to act according to their unique methodology to sustain a healthy relationship. However, some clashes are bound to happen between people of different personality types.

Chapter 10: Finding Your Perfectionist Growth Path

Type 1 Enneagram perfectionists are the most conscientious and hard-working of all Enneagram types. However, they can also be highly stressed individuals because of the high expectations they have, as we have read in the past chapters. Enneagram Type 1 can become a healthy Enneagram type by giving themselves permission to take time off from their perfectionism and learn how to relax.

Integrating Direction Relies on Intent

As per the Enneagram theory, when 1 starts Disintegrating or moving towards stress, their growth regresses. Leading a stressed, unfulfilled life affects all aspects of your being - relationships, career, and overall peace and happiness. However, with focused intent, you can quickly move toward integration - health and growth.

There are many different reasons why someone might have an unhealthy, unbalanced personality, and it doesn't take long before they start suffering from anxiety or depression. Integrating direction relies on intent and also helps people learn how to be more grounded in themselves so they can reach their full potential as human beings.

In this chapter, we will discuss your growth journey in detail.

Areas of Improvement for Type 1 Personalities

Type 1 personalities are inherent perfectionists. They are hard on themselves to do the right things and expect no less from the world around them. Anything out of place makes them uncomfortable. Enneagram Type 1 personalities need to develop a more flexible attitude towards life and learn how to embrace imperfections in order to become healthy individuals.

Here are some common inherent traits that perfectionists need to acknowledge:

The Demand for Perfection and Idealism

Type 1s set high standards for others, but they also expect the same of themselves and become stressed when things don't go as planned or expected.

Judgmental and Self-Critical

Judgmental and Self-Critical Type 1s are their own worst critic, who makes them very hard on themselves in all areas of life.

Difficulty Expressing Their Needs

Type 1s often sacrifice what they need for the sake of order in their lives, which can lead to high levels of stress and burnout. They need to learn how to express their needs and take the initiative in order to lead a healthy life.

Perfectionistic Parental Expectations

Type 1 is often raised by parents who have high expectations for their child, which can leave them confused and unsure how to meet these high expectations, so they end up insecure and doubting their self-worth.

Increased Frustrations because of Imperfections in the World

Easily frustrated, this personality is often frustrated with the imperfections in life, adding to an already heavy stress burden.

Not Acknowledging Frustration and Anger

The Type-1 personality doesn't acknowledge their anger and frustration, which can lead to them feeling resentful.

Problems Caused by a Very Loud Conscience

Type 1 Reformers have a very loud conscience and internal dialogue. They find it hard to ignore what they feel guilty about, which causes them to obsess over their imperfections even more than usual and often carry the weight of guilt on their shoulders for most of their lives.

By learning how to become self-aware, you can start changing the way you react toward things that trigger stress and frustration so you can begin to lead a healthier life. You also need to take responsibility for yourself by identifying your needs and desires as well as what is realistic for you.

Self-Improvement Tips

Type 1 personalities need to take responsibility for themselves and identify their needs. They also have to learn how to relax in order to prevent feeling overwhelmed by stressing all of the time.

Practice a daily routine that enhances relaxation, including taking a warm bath with lavender oil, using self-massage techniques on your feet or hands, going for a walk in nature, listening to music, light reading, and yoga.

You should also learn not to over-commit or set unrealistic expectations.

By becoming aware of your limitations and needs, you can start doing things in a healthier way that will help you work toward achieving long-term growth.

Take care to develop self-love instead of comparing yourself against others all the time.

You should also try to let go of absolute perfectionism because it does not exist (in fact). Perfection is subjective, and it varies from person to person.

It is essential for the type 1 personality types to acknowledge their anger instead of immediately repressing it, as they can start feeling resentful towards others.

If you are a Type 1 who has a hard time expressing your feelings or needs, learning how to communicate them can reduce stress levels and help you to feel better in your everyday life.

Becoming aware of the things that trigger anger or frustration is essential because it gives you a chance to learn how not to react towards them in the future.

Developing self-love instead of constantly feeling guilty for not being good enough can also help you achieve long-term growth and wellness in your life.

Self-Reflection Questions for Perfectionists: Should you change?

Type 1 personalities are known to strive to do anything they do to an impossibly perfect standard and suffer if they think they haven't reached that bar.

Self-reflection and questioning your motives and emotions are vital, so you get a chance to learn how not to react toward things that trigger anger or frustration so as not to lead a healthier life.

- •Do you feel irritable by slight imperfections around you?

- •Do you think that people around you just cannot do anything right?

- •Do you get angry at yourself because you could not deliver on your own expectations?

•Are you unable to enjoy little joys in life and always feel a wanting for something more?

•Does your conscience constantly tell you that you are not doing enough?

•Do you think that to be loved, you must be perfect and improvement-oriented?

•Do you find yourself judging those around you constantly?

If you answer yes to most of these questions, there is a need to start working on yourself to lead a better, fulfilling, and non-judgmental life. You need to take responsibility for yourself, learn to find peace in imperfections, and above all, learn forgiveness.

Opportunities for Growth: Perfectionists/Reformers

Your Perfectionist personality benefits immensely from your principled, disciplined, and goal-oriented way of life. This helps you build successful careers and maintain honest relationships. You are also the proverbial policemen our society needs - those who do the right thing and force those around them to also do the right thing.

However, the burden of these values is the expectation of perfection from an imperfect world. Often leading to an unfulfilled life. Try to follow the practical tips in the section below to get on the path of a more fulfilling life.

Understand that the World is Not Perfect

Accept Imperfections of the World around you and learn to find peace in being flawed. This will help lead a healthier life overall and have more time for self-reflection instead of constantly feeling guilty about things that are not your fault.

Learn how to be less judgmental towards yourself as well as others.

Be kind to yourself and others- this will allow you to live a happier, less stressful life.

Permit Yourself to Stray from Your Beliefs

It is perfectly okay if you sleep in for a few extra minutes - the world will not collapse. Appreciate the spare time and thank the universe for the opportunity of living another day.

Going against your ideals of absolute morality is okay in a delicate situation. Accepting that not everything is black and white and that every case deserves a just and appropriate response from you is critical. You have to learn to adapt to challenging situations where you will have to improvise your behavior, hold your judgment, and concur with the problem in a mature way.

Control Your Inner Critical Voice

You need to learn from the above paragraph and implement it in your life. This is an arduous task, but an essential one because you will only be able to lead a happier life if you can control this inner critic who loves nothing more than tearing apart everything that comes before their eyes.

Learn how not to react towards things that trigger anger or frustration so as not to lead a healthier life.

Affirmations for Enneagram Type1 Perfectionists

- I am self-sufficient.

- I need no one's approval to be happy or content with myself.

- It is okay if I have flaws, they will only serve to make me a stronger person in life.

- Opinions of people around me are not necessary for my happiness. It is perfectly alright for me to disagree and be different.

- I am enough. I do not need to be perfect for anyone or anything in the world.

- My body is strong and healthy - it will help me live another day on this planet.

- Forgiveness is an integral part of my life - I must learn how to forgive myself as well as others who have hurt me in the past.

- I am not above anyone else, as every person deserves an opportunity to find happiness and live a fulfilling life.

- It is okay if I do not understand something immediately - there are many things that will take some time for me to comprehend, but I must learn how to be patient with myself.

- The world is a beautiful place, filled with many different people.

- The world is not perfect - but it can be an excellent place when I learn to accept its imperfections and live in the moment.

- I must learn from my mistakes - instead of dwelling on them or letting them fester inside me for too long.

- I am not above anyone else - Every person deserves an opportunity to live a happy life.

- It is okay if my goals are different from those around me - we all have our own paths in this world, which means there will always be people who think differently from us.

- I will do what I can to help other people, but it is vital that I first and foremost take care of myself.

- It is okay if my life does not look like a picture-perfect Instagram feed - there are many different types of beauty in this world which means we must learn how to embrace the things that make us unique.

- I will set goals that are achievable and doable. I cannot stress myself by setting unrealistic expectations for myself.

• It is okay if things don't go my way sometimes. What seems like a bad situation on the outside may be an opportunity in disguise to learn something new.

• I am not alone in this world. I have the support of my family and friends to get me through the tough times.

• I am not above anyone else. Every person deserves an opportunity to live a happy life.

Daily Routines for Growth

Meditation and Yoga

One of the best ways to de-stress and clear your mind is meditating. It will allow you to take some time away from all your worries and focus on yourself without judgment or stress. Yoga is another excellent way to clear your mind and get yourself centered. You can do this by yourself at home or join a group class.

Be Patient with Yourself and Others

Since perfectionists are usually very self-critical, it is crucial that you learn how to be patient with not only yourself but also with other people around you who may be struggling as well. You must realize that everyone makes mistakes every so often- including yourself.

Learn to Forgive Yourself and Others

Forgiveness is an essential part of life. You must learn how to forgive yourself for your mistakes without holding on or dwelling on them. You also must try and forgive others who have hurt you in the past so that they may be able to move forward with their lives as well.

Learn to Appreciate the Small Things

The little things are what make up our daily routines, and learning to appreciate these small moments will not only bring you joy – but also teach you how to be grateful for all that you have in life. It is essential to take time each day and reflect on everything around us instead of focusing too much on materialistic items.

Learn How to Live in the Moment

It is crucial that you learn how to live for the moment but also appreciate all of the small things around us. You must learn how to take care of yourself before worrying about others- this means taking time out for yourself, doing something creative, and setting goals so you can work towards achieving them.

Embrace Imperfections

The world is not perfect, but it can be an excellent place when you learn to accept its imperfections and live in the moment. You must understand that you cannot control everything around you, no matter how hard you try. This means learning how to let go of certain things so that they may have a chance to grow and thrive.

Be True to Yourself

It is vital that I am true to myself. Understand your needs, work toward getting them fulfilled, listen to what you want, and don't only rely on your rules and methods. It will help to set realistic goals and work towards them honestly.

Take Care of Yourself and Others

It is vital that I take care of myself, and this means finding a healthy balance between work, family, and friends.

Set Goals and Learn from Mistakes

You must learn to set goals for yourself and work toward achieving them. This means learning from your mistakes, being patient with those around you who are struggling as well as forgiving others instead of holding a grudge against them.

Be Thankful for the Small Things

It is essential that I take time each day to be thankful. This means learning how to live in the moment, setting goals so you can work towards achieving them, and most importantly, taking care of yourself before worrying about others. Be thankful for the life you have been given, for the people in it, and the motivation to live every day.

Take Care of Yourself First

It does not always work to look after others' needs. It is important that you understand your needs - emotional and physical. Work towards achieving your needs without guilt or without the need to be the social messiah. Everybody is entitled to their own space.

Live with Gratitude

It is not about living perfectly but instead learning how to be grateful for the things around you no matter what they may be because it will allow you to live life to the fullest.

These suggestions would be extremely helpful for a Type 1 Perfectionist to follow. It's a growth plan to help you understand how to live with gratitude and appreciation for the small things in life. Learning to be patient with others, forgiving yourself when you make a mistake or fail, embracing an imperfect world- are essential steps that will allow you to thrive and grow into who it is you want to become.

Be sure to set goals for yourself, take care of yourself before worrying about others, and most importantly, learn how to let go so you can appreciate those around you. Type 1 will not succeed if they try to control everything but instead must embrace the world as it is – a beautiful yet imperfect place.

By taking time each day to be thankful for the small things in life, you will learn how to live with gratitude and without regret or worry. This is an important step that Type 1s must take if they want to succeed. They must learn how to forgive themselves when they make a mistake, be patient with others who are struggling and embrace their own imperfections.

Conclusion

In this book, through the various chapters, we have explored the Perfectionist Enneagram. We have seen that the Perfectionist is hard-working and conscientious, making them excellent employees or managers. The same attention to detail often makes them good teachers as well. They are serious about their responsibilities and can be overly harsh on themselves when things do not go according to plan. This has contributed to their identity of always being "in control." The Perfectionist can also be overly critical of others, which makes them hard to get along with sometimes.

In other chapters, we explored how unhealthy 1s begin to fall into a path of disintegration that leads toward unhappiness, stress, neurosis, and even psychosis. This is where they become increasingly self-centered and paranoid about their actions and intentions as well as those of others. This self-focus causes them to become increasingly reclusive and withdrawn from society, as they don't want people around who might not see their "true" character or intentions; the result is that few really know what goes on behind closed doors or inside the mind of a 1. They are hard-working individuals but begin to push away any who might actually appreciate their efforts.

We went on to discuss the Healthy 1s and how they can most often be found in the company of those who are part of their "inner circle" or close friends. This is where 1s begin to loosen up and actually feel more at ease around others, especially when it comes to discussing matters that may not always go according to plan. Healthy 1s appreciate this acceptance and love from people close to them, which often leads to them being more open and receptive to the love they receive from others.

The next chapter explored the Type 1 Wing 9 — The Idealist. These types are very similar in many ways but can also have a few key differences that set them apart. Their self-discipline is strong, and they may sometimes be overly critical of others. However, they often experience more mood swings than their Type 1 counterparts and can become easily overwhelmed by the emotions that surface at times. These individuals are also very hard-working, but this is usually in service to a greater cause or "higher power."

Similarly, The Activists are even more easily overwhelmed by their emotions. They can also make impulsive decisions; however, this desire for change is usually motivated by something larger than themselves and the need to do what's right or appropriate in a given situation.

Relationships with other types of Enneagram Personalities can be challenging for the Perfectionist. They are often seen as too rigid or critical, leading to others not wanting to be around them. However, their hard-working and conscientious nature makes these individuals great friends once they feel like someone is trustworthy enough for a relationship with the 1.

Perfectionists are the complete package - strong morals and ideals, a deep sense of right and wrong, and an overwhelming need to get things just right. However, thanks to their extreme nature, they walk the thin line between healthy and unhealthy tendencies. If you are a perfectionist or know someone who is one, take heart in knowing that there is hope for change. With time and effort, it's possible to overcome your unhealthy tendencies and live with more peace, wholeness, and more deep satisfaction from life!

Here's another book by Mari Silva that you might like

MARI SILVA

AIR MAGIC

HARNESSING THIS NATURAL ELEMENT IN WITCHCRAFT AND MAGIC USING SPELLS, CRYSTALS, RITUALS, HERBS, MEDITATION, ASTRAL TRAVEL, AND TOTEMS ALONG WITH HOW TO CONNECT WITH ANIMAL SPIRIT GUIDES

Your Free Gift (only available for a limited time)

Thanks for getting this book! If you want to learn more about various spirituality topics, then join Mari Silva's community and get a free guided meditation MP3 for awakening your third eye. This guided meditation mp3 is designed to open and strengthen ones third eye so you can experience a higher state of consciousness. Simply visit the link below the image to get started.

https://spiritualityspot.com/meditation

References

How the system works — the enneagram institute. (n.d.). Enneagraminstitute.Com.

The 3 instincts from the enneagram. (2016, July 11). Lifetime.Life. https://experiencelife.lifetime.life/article/basic-insincts/

Three Centres of Intelligence. (n.d.). Theenneagramsingapore.Com. Retrieved from https://www.theenneagramsingapore.com/three-centres-of-intelligence/

What is the Enneagram of personality? (2019, August 8). Truity.Com. https://www.truity.com/enneagram/what-is-enneagram

(N.d.). Coralvilleumc.Org.

Enneagram 1 - The Perfectionist. (n.d.). Narrativeenneagram.Org. Retrieved from https://www.narrativeenneagram.org/types/the-perfectionist/

Famous people with the Enneagram 1 personality type. (n.d.). Crystalknows.Com.

Instinctual Subtypes. (n.d.). Narrativeenneagram.Org. Retrieved from https://www.narrativeenneagram.org/instinctual-subtypes/

Three Centres of Intelligence. (n.d.). Theenneagramsingapore.Com. Retrieved from https://www.theenneagramsingapore.com/three-centres-of-intelligence/

Type 1. (n.d.). Fitzel.Ca. Retrieved from http://www.fitzel.ca/enneagram/Type1.html

Enneagram Type 1: The Perfectionist. (2019, August 8). Retrieved from Truity.com website: https://www.truity.com/enneagram/personality-type-1-perfectionist

Stafford, S. (2020, August 8). Enneagram Type 1 strengths, Talents, and skills: How enneagram Type 1 excels. Retrieved from Personalitygrowth.com website: https://personalitygrowth.com/enneagram-type-1-strengths-talents-and-skills-how-enneagram-type-one-excels/

Type 1 careers. (2020, May 7). Retrieved from Thecareerproject.org website: https://www.thecareerproject.org/personality-type/type-1/

(N.d.). Retrieved from Russellrowe.com website: http://www.russellrowe.com/enneagram-types/enneagram-type-1-description.pdf

Enneagram Type 1. (n.d.). Retrieved from Yourenneagramcoach.com website: https://www.yourenneagramcoach.com/type1

Hedley, J. (n.d.). Strengths and Struggles of the 9 Enneagram Types. Retrieved from Com.au website: https://www.thecoachingroom.com.au/blog/strengths-and-struggles-of-the-9-enneagram-types

McCormick, J. E. (2018, November 19). Each enneagram type's biggest fear and what to do about it. Retrieved from Relevantmagazine.com website: https://www.relevantmagazine.com/culture/each-enneagram-types-biggest-fear-and-what-to-do-about-it/

Morin, A. (2014, November 6). Taming your inner critic: 7 steps to silencing the negativity. Forbes Magazine. Retrieved from https://www.forbes.com/sites/amymorin/2014/11/06/taming-your-inner-critic-7-steps-to-silencing-the-negativity/

Storm, S., & Yuan, L. (2018, October 4). Here's what you fear, based on your enneagram type. Retrieved from Psychologyjunkie.com website: https://www.psychologyjunkie.com/2018/10/04/heres-what-you-fear-based-on-your-enneagram-type/

(N.d.). Retrieved from Russellrowe.com website: http://www.russellrowe.com/enneagram-types/enneagram-type-1-description.pdf

Enneagram: Directions of Integration (Growth) and Disintegration (Stress). (2017, January 31). Retrieved from Marikamessager.com website: https://www.marikamessager.com/enneagram-directions-of-integration-growth-and-disintegration-stress/

Garrison, C. (2020, August 13). 7 signs that Enneagram 1's are slipping into an unhealthy place.

Hall, S. B. (2020, April 20). Enneagram Movement Points. Retrieved from Ninetypes.co website: https://ninetypes.co/blog/enneagram-movement-points

J1's, S. (2018, June 7). Enneagram disintegration: Keys to solving overthinking. Retrieved from Introvertedalpha.com website: https://introvertedalpha.com/enneagram-growth/

Levels of Development. (n.d.). Retrieved from Theenneagramsingapore.com website: https://www.theenneagramsingapore.com/levels-of-development/

Stafford, S. (2020, July 13). Enneagram Type 1 Under Stress: Enneagram Type 1 Moving in the Direction of disintegration. Retrieved from Personalitygrowth.com website: https://personalitygrowth.com/enneagram-type-1-under-stress-enneagram-type-one-moving-in-the-direction-of-disintegration/

Storm, S. (2020, November 7). Signs that you're disintegrating, based on your Enneagram type. Retrieved from Psychologyjunkie.com website: https://www.psychologyjunkie.com/2020/11/07/signs-that-youre-disintegrating-based-on-your-enneagram-type/

Storm, S., & Yuan, L. (2019, April 22). Here's what you're like on a bad day, based on your Enneagram type. Retrieved from Psychologyjunkie.com website: https://www.psychologyjunkie.com/2019/04/22/heres-what-youre-like-on-a-bad-day-based-on-your-enneagram-type/

Storm, S., & Yuan, L. (2020a, June 2). 10 signs of an unhealthy Enneagram One. Retrieved from Psychologyjunkie.com website: https://www.psychologyjunkie.com/2020/06/02/10-signs-of-an-unhealthy-enneagram-one/

Storm, S., & Yuan, L. (2020b, August 6). Integration, disintegration, and your enneagram type. Retrieved from Psychologyjunkie.com website: https://www.psychologyjunkie.com/2020/08/06/enneagram-integration-disintegration/

(N.d.). Retrieved from Linkedin.com website: https://www.linkedin.com/pulse/moving-up-levels-development-enneagram-belinda-gore

Cloete, D. (n.d.-a). Enneagram Type 1. Retrieved from Integrative9.com website: https://www.integrative9.com/enneagram/introduction/type-1/

Cloete, D. (n.d.-b). Wings, arrow lines, integration, and self-mastery. Retrieved from Integrative9.com website: https://www.integrative9.com/enneagram/wings-lines-integration/

Crystal - Enneagram Type 1 and Enneagram Type 7 Relationship. (n.d.). Retrieved from Crystalknows.com website: https://www.crystalknows.com/enneagram/type-1/relationship/enneagram/type-7

Enneagram: Directions of Integration (Growth) and Disintegration (Stress). (2017, January 31). Retrieved from Marikamessager.com website: https://www.marikamessager.com/enneagram-directions-of-integration-growth-and-disintegration-stress/

Hall, S. B. (2020, April 20). Enneagram Movement Points. Retrieved from Ninetypes.co website: https://ninetypes.co/blog/enneagram-movement-points

How the system works — the enneagram institute. (n.d.). Retrieved from Enneagraminstitute.com website: https://www.enneagraminstitute.com/how-the-enneagram-system-works

melissakircher. (2018, March 26). Enneagram Type 1: Basic Characteristics and arrows » enneagram paths. Retrieved from Enneagrampaths.com website: https://enneagrampaths.com/2018/03/26/enneagram-type-one-basic-characterisitcs-and-arrows/

Pinterest. (n.d.). Retrieved from Pinterest.com website: https://in.pinterest.com/pin/515099276107771938/visual-search/?x=16&y=12&w=530&h=397

Storm, S., & Yuan, L. (2020a, March 16). The best and worst versions of every enneagram type. Retrieved from Psychologyjunkie.com website: https://www.psychologyjunkie.com/2020/03/16/the-best-and-worst-versions-of-every-enneagram-type/

Storm, S., & Yuan, L. (2020b, August 6). Integration, disintegration, and your enneagram type. Retrieved from Psychologyjunkie.com website: https://www.psychologyjunkie.com/2020/08/06/enneagram-integration-disintegration/

Type 1 — The Enneagram Institute. (n.d.). Retrieved from Enneagraminstitute.com website: https://www.enneagraminstitute.com/type-1

Type 7 — The Enneagram Institute. (n.d.). Retrieved from Enneagraminstitute.com website: https://www.enneagraminstitute.com/type-7

(N.d.-a). Retrieved from Personalitycafe.com website: https://www.personalitycafe.com/threads/integrating-to-7.145177/#post-3684637

(N.d.-b). Retrieved from Linkedin.com website: https://www.linkedin.com/pulse/moving-up-levels-development-enneagram-belinda-gore

(N.d.-c). Retrieved from Personalitycafe.com website: https://www.personalitycafe.com/threads/type- 1-integration.1215866/

Enneagram 1w9: The one with a9-wing. (n.d.). Psychologia.Co. Retrieved from https://psychologia.co/1w9/

Enneagram Type 1w9 - The Optimist. (n.d.). Crystalknows.Com. Retrieved from https://www.crystalknows.com/enneagram/type-1/wing-9

Enneagram Type 1w9: Childhood (A complete guide) - PsychReel. (n.d.). Psychreel.Com. Retrieved from https://psychreel.com/enneagram-type-1w9-childhood/

Interpreting your enneagram test results — the enneagram institute. (n.d.). Enneagraminstitute.Com. Retrieved from https://www.enneagraminstitute.com/interpreting-your-enneagram-test-results

Samuel. (2021, May 22). Enneagram 1w9 Personality and Best Jobs for them. Howigotjob.Com. https://howigotjob.com/articles/enneagram-1w9-personality/

Storm, S. (2020, March 10). The childhood wounds of every enneagram type. Psychologyjunkie.Com. https://www.psychologyjunkie.com/2020/03/10/the-childhood-wounds-of-every-enneagram-type/

Turner, N. (2018, August 20).Type 1 with 9 wing. Intuitive-Enneagram.Com. https://intuitive-enneagram.com/2018/08/20/type-1-with-nine-wing/

Type 1 careers. (2020, May 7). Thecareerproject.Org. https://www.thecareerproject.org/personality-type/type-1/

1w2 careers (A guide). (n.d.). Psychreel.Com. Retrieved from https://psychreel.com/1w2-careers/

Enneagram type 1, the Reformer: Best and worst careers. (n.d.). Fairygodboss.Com. Retrieved from https://fairygodboss.com/career-topics/enneagram-type-1-careers

Enneagram Type 1w2 - The Activist. (n.d.). Crystalknows.Com. Retrieved from https://www.crystalknows.com/enneagram/type-1/wing-2

Enneagram Type 1w2: Childhood (A complete guide) - PsychReel. (n.d.). Psychreel.Com. Retrieved from https://psychreel.com/enneagram-type-1w2-childhood/

Life as an enneagram 1w2 - Danielle Ripley-Burgess. (2019, January 8). Danielleripleyburgess.Com. https://www.danielleripleyburgess.com/about/life-as-an-enneagram-1w2/

melissakircher. (2020, February 17). Enneagram type 1w9 vs. 1w2 » enneagram paths. Enneagrampaths.Com. https://enneagrampaths.com/2020/02/17/enneagram-type-1w9-vs-1w2/

Sarikas, C. (n.d.). Enneagram type 1: The perfectionist in life, love, and work. Prepscholar.Com. Retrieved from https://blog.prepscholar.com/enneagram-type-1

Relationship type 1 with type 1 — the enneagram institute. (n.d.). Enneagraminstitute.Com. Retrieved from https://www.enneagraminstitute.com/relationship-type-1-with-type-1

The Enneagram types in relationship. (2015, July 11). Drdaviddaniels.Com. Retrieved from https://drdaviddaniels.com/relationships-intimacy/enneagram-types-in-relationship/

Enneagram compatibility Type 1 with Type 1 / Lynn Roulo. (2018, October 29). Lynnroulo.Com. Retrieved from https://www.lynnroulo.com/about/enneagram/enneagram-type-combinations/perfectionist-1-with-perfectionist-1/

Sarikas, C. (n.d.). Enneagram type 1: The perfectionist in life, love, and work. Prepscholar.Com. Retrieved from https://blog.prepscholar.com/enneagram-type-1

Storm, S. (2020, September 9). Here's what you need in a friendship, based on your enneagram type. Psychologyjunkie.Com. Retrieved from https://www.psychologyjunkie.com/2020/09/09/heres-what-you-need-in-a-friendship-based-on-your-enneagram-type/

Enneagram 1 - The Perfectionist. (n.d.). Narrativeenneagram.Org. Retrieved from https://www.narrativeenneagram.org/types/the-perfectionist/

Enneagram type 1: Positive affirmations for path of growth. (2015, October 19). Evelynlim.Com. https://www.evelynlim.com/enneagram-type-1-positive-affirmations-for-path-of-growth/

Enneagram Type 1: The Perfectionist. (2019, August 8). Truity.Com. https://www.truity.com/enneagram/personality-type-1-perfectionist

Growth Enneagram Type 1. (2012, July 5). Drdaviddaniels.Com. https://drdaviddaniels.com/growth-for-type-1/

How the system works — the enneagram institute. (n.d.). Enneagraminstitute.Com. Retrieved from https://www.enneagraminstitute.com/how-the-enneagram-system-works

Lindsy. (2019, October 8). Enneagram Type 1 growth: Mantras for transformation — BREATHE + GLOW. Breatheandglow.Com; BREATHE + GLOW. http://breatheandglow.com/myblog/2019/10/6/enneagram-type-1-growth-10-mantras-for-an-enneagram-type-one